BR

MW00438707

THINGS FALL APART BY CHINUA ACHEBE

Intelligent Education

INFLUENCE PUBLISHERS

Nashville, Tennessee

BRIGHT NOTES: Things Fall Apart

www.BrightNotes.com

No part of this publication may be used or reproduced in any manner whatsoever without written permission, except in the case of brief quotations in critical articles and reviews. For permissions, contact Influence Publishers http://www.influencepublishers.com.

ISBN: 978-1-645420-62-0 (Paperback)
ISBN: 978-1-645420-63-7 (eBook)

Published in accordance with the U.S. Copyright Office Orphan Works and Mass Digitization report of the register of copyrights, June 2015.

Originally published by Monarch Press.
Steven H. Gale, 1990
2019 Edition published by Influence Publishers.

Interior design by Lapiz Digital Services. Cover Design by Thinkpen Designs.

Printed in the United States of America.

Library of Congress Cataloging-in-Publication Data forthcoming.
Names: Intelligent Education
Title: BRIGHT NOTES: Things Fall Apart
Subject: STU004000 STUDY AIDS / Book Notes

CONTENTS

INTRODUCTION TO THINGS FALL APART

A STORY WITH UNIVERSAL APPEAL

Like any work of true art, *Things Fall Apart* can stand on its own, needing no study of historical background, literary history, anthropology, or current sociological concepts to make it meaningful. Plot, character development, **theme**, and overall style (use of language, structure, and so forth) are all strong enough to hold the reader's interest, and it meets Horace's criteria for great literature by being both entertaining and enlightening. Achebe is foremost a superb story-teller and the story that he tells contains universal elements so that it has a continuing meaning for people in times and cultures beyond that in which and about which it was written.

ANTHROPOLOGICAL AND SOCIOLOGICAL ELEMENTS

On the other hand, it would be foolish to ignore certain levels of meaning in the book that give it added impact, reinforce its statements, or explain some of its nuances. Much of Achebe's work, for example, has been the subject of studies with a decidedly anthropological or sociological bias, as opposed to a literary one. These elements are inherent in the tales and give anthropologists and sociologists' glimpses into a culture that they might otherwise never experience - glimpses provided by one who is aware of the difference between the culture that he writes of and the culture that he is, at least in part, writing to. The anthropological and sociological examinations and discussions of Achebe's tales also give the student of literature a wider perspective for understanding both the content of the novels and the author's choice of techniques for expressing himself. For instance, R. Green's "The Clashing of Old and New" (*The Nation*, CCL, II, 1965) might prove useful for an interdisciplinary point of view, and, while limited, *The Literature and Thought of Modern Africa* (London, 1966) by Claude Wauthier is also of interest.

EARLY NIGERIAN CULTURES

For the fullest understanding of Achebe's *Things Fall Apart*, it is worthwhile to trace certain historical facts and to examine pertinent aspects of Nigerian (or, rather, Ibo) culture, and then to review other African writing to gain a better appreciation of the scope of the author's achievement, an achievement that becomes startlingly clear when his work is compared with that of his continental contemporaries. To begin, it is useful to consider that Nigeria has not always been a developing Third-World country, as it is perceived today. As early as 700 B.C., there were established cultures in the area. From about 500 B.C. to 200 A.D., the Iron Age Nok culture flourished on the Benue Plateau - this was during the time that Alexander the Great was creating the greatest empire yet seen in the Western world, and most of Europe was still in a primitive tribal state. Later, during the twelfth through the fourteenth centuries, advanced cultures appeared in the Yoruba area and in the north (where Muslim influence was felt), and the Ife terra cottas were among the finest examples of that art form ever created.

EUROPEAN CONTACT

West Africa has had contact of one sort or another with Europe for many centuries. There is evidence of trade goods being imported from the Mediterranean area even during the time of the great African kingdoms, and trade was well established by the European Middle Ages. For obvious reasons, there was little interest in European countries regarding annexation of African colonies until better transportation and communication systems were developed and until there were trade goods that made the effort worth the cost economically.

SLAVERY

In West Africa, the two major sources of British interest were gold and slaves, and Nigeria was to become one of the major slave-supplying areas of all Africa. There had been slavery in Africa long before the arrival of the British, of course; there was a limited amount of slavery practiced among the blacks from prehistoric times, a practice that Achebe alludes to in his novels, and this practice was expanded greatly by the Arab nations to the North. The first instance of Europeans becoming involved in the slave trade was in 1441 when a Portuguese vessel returned to Lisbon from an exploratory expedition with twelve slaves. Within a few years, the number of slaves being taken from Africa reached the thousands.

"MAN-MONEY"

Portuguese and British slavers visited Nigeria as early as the fifteenth century, and it was the slave trade that stimulated English interest in the country, though not until the sixteenth and seventeenth centuries when the trade was at its height. At one point in the early nineteenth century, in fact, Lagos was the largest slave depot in the region. Ironically, in 1807 England passed a law declaring the slave trade illegal and after that her interest in things African waned, although during an anti-slavery campaign Britain seized Lagos (in 1861), and continuing conflict with France led to a series of treaties between 1890 and 1898 that settled various boundary disputes. An interesting relic of slave-trading can still be found in Africa today in the form of the beaten black iron rods that were formerly used for money. The "country-money," as the rods are now called, is long and thin and twisted, like wrought iron, with the two ends being beaten flat, roundly wide at one end, sharply triangle-shaped at the other. The value of the rod is determined by its length (in the mid-1970s, for example, a piece from twelve to fifteen inches long and about an eighth to a quarter of an inch thick was worth one or two American cents). A huge, heavy iron rod, four to five feet in length, was called "man-money" because it could be used to buy a man.

BRITISH COLONIAL SYSTEM

Leaving aside any question of morality, the British system of colonization traditionally has been more moderate and humane than most others. This system was based on two things: (1) the general English attitude toward its colonies and its responsibilities to those colonies (at least in part fostered by their experiences in America), and (2) the educational system set up within the colonized country to train native clerical workers and civil service employees ("Nigeria boasts more university graduates than any other African nation," according to a *Newsweek* cover story, "Nigeria: The First Black Power," March 4, 1974, p. 13). "In West Africa," George H. T. Kimble says in *Tropical Africa* (New York: Twentieth-Century Fund, 1960), "Britain assumed minimum responsibilities and developed an efficient and inexpensive system to govern a large area." This was the system of "indirect rule": "that policy of allowing the powers of traditional rulers to remain intact to the maximum degree consonant with imperial rule" (Immanuel Wallerstein, Africa: The Politics of Independence, New York: Random House, 1961). In Nigeria this pattern was instituted by Lord Lugard in 1914. After World War II Britain was among the leading powers to accept the legitimacy of the "objective of national independence," and the rapid transfer of power to the native populations - with a minimum of violence and antagonism - was admirable.

NIGERIAN INDEPENDENCE

Because of the attitude of Great Britain toward her colonies, she was not adverse to granting them independence and, indeed, often made the metamorphosis as easy as possible by encouraging the development of a federal form of government. As mentioned above, the ease of this political change was partly due to the British system of providing a responsibility-sharing program and an education system which prepared the new nation's leaders for the transference. From 1946 through 1958, the Nigerians moved toward a multi-party, parliamentary-type government as they framed their constitution. On October 1, 1960, an independent nation was proclaimed within the British Commonwealth. Three years later, on October 1, 1963, the first nationwide elections were held as Nigeria became a republic.

Colonization certainly had taken its toll in human terms, however, and it is perhaps at least partly for this reason that the Biafran question arose in 1966 and that the military government, led by General Yakubu Dan Yumma "Jack" Gowon, came to rule. The task of welding sixty-five million people, comprising 250 different tribes, into one nation seemed almost impossible when Gowon came to power, after the second coup in seven months, to establish a "military democracy." But, "Guided by highly trained technocrats who were one of the better legacies of the British colonial period, the Nigerian civil service continued to function ably throughout the upheavals of the 1960s" (*Newsweek*, "Nigeria: The First Black Power," March 4, 1974, p. 10) and Gowon proved a more competent, sensible, and sincere leader than had been expected. The announced intention was for Gowon to step aside in favor of a civilian government, though there was considerable speculation as to whether the country was ready for such a method of self-rule. Still, Gowon was replaced by a peaceful return to civilian government in October 1979, for it was generally believed that he would not have been willing to see his achievements destroyed and might have decided to retain control. Unfortunately, the democratically elected government was ousted in a coup on December 31, 1983, and military rule has returned. General Ibrahim Babangida assumed the position of head of state on August 30, 1985; the government promised that democratic rule would be instituted by 1992.

ACHEBE'S ATTITUDES

As it must be under the circumstances, Achebe's writing is concerned with colonialism and the effect of colonialism on the native Nigerian, though it certainly would not be valid to claim that this is all that he writes about. It is interesting, therefore, to explore his feelings about Nigeria's colonial and post-colonial periods. As might be expected, the writer's attitude reflects feelings of ambiguity.

Moderate in comparison with many African political leaders, Achebe's opinion is not "that Africa has gained nothing at all during the colonial period .... But unfortunately when two cultures meet ... [what often happens] is that some of the worst elements of the old are retained and some of the worst of the new are added" (Quoted in Robert Serumaga's "Interview with Achebe," *Cultural Events in Africa*, 28, Transcription Center, London, 1967).

Elsewhere, Achebe is even more pessimistic:

... in her long encounter with Europe, [Africa] ... suffered many terrible and lasting misfortunes. In terms of human dignity and human relations, the encounter was almost a complete disaster for the black races. It has warped the mental attitudes of both black and white.

("The Black Writer's Burden," *Presence Africaine*, Paris, 1962, p. 135)

Achebe has also seen the encounter in a more optimistic light on occasion:

... I believe that in political and economic terms ... this arbitrary creation called Nigeria [created by the intervention of the British] holds out wonderful prospects. Yet the fact remains that Nigeria was created by the British - for her own ends. Let us give the devil his due: Colonialism in Africa disrupted many things, but it did create big political units where there were small scattered ones before ... Of course there are areas of Africa where colonialism divided a single ethnic group among two or even three powers. But on the whole it did bring together many that had hitherto gone their several ways.

("The English Language and the African Writer," *Insight*, October/December, 1966, pp. 19–20)

Among the unifying elements that Achebe details (discussed below) is the imposing of English on diverse native populations as a common - albeit second-language. This, he states, is a major contribution leftover from the colonial period.

IBO PERSPECTIVE

At the same time, Achebe's heritage as an Ibo tribesman has given him an added perspective. The traditional Ibo government structure is not the same as that of the other tribes with which the British dealt, and the differences precipitated many of the conflicts that the writer describes in his novels (most notably in *Things Fall Apart* and *Arrow of God*). Even when this basic distinction is not the explicit focus of Achebe's writing, as in *No Longer at Ease*, it is still an important part of the background. William R. Bascom and Melville J. Herskovits have described the conventional native political system, which allowed the British system to be incorporated with such facility, as contrasted with the governmental structure of the Ibo people, in *Continuity and Change in African Cultures* (Chicago: University of Chicago Press, 1959):

Nigeria affords a classic example of the effect of cultural backgrounds on the course of recent history. The policy of indirect rule was first applied among the Hausa in the north, where political authority was centered in the Emir [an Arabic influence] and where taxation, courts, and other governmental institutions comparable to those of Europe were already in existence. It was extended with little difficulty to the Yoruba in the southwest, since their

traditional political structure was sufficiently similar. But the attempt to apply it to the Ibo in the southeast failed because comparable political units on which to superimpose the new systems were lacking.

According to Margaret Laurence in *Long Drums and Cannons* (London: Macmillan, 1968), those political units were lacking because: "Although the Ibo number some five million people, they never had any central organization or any kings. Their tribal setup was markedly different from most tribal societies because of its individualism and its rejections of any inherited or hierarchical system of authority" (page 98).

M. M. Green's *Ibo Village Affairs* (New York: Praeger, 1964) gives a more picturesque and less theoretical view of life among the Ibo.

NIGERIAN CORRUPTION

Outside his own villages - that is to say, in most of Nigeria and in Lagos - the Ibo tribesman is made especially aware of the differences which surround him, and, as is the case with Obi Okonkwo, the **protagonist** of *No Longer at Ease*, the tribesman often finds himself in a degenerate culture. Obi's repulsion at the corruption of Lagos in general and government officials in particular is not surprising, then. Nor is that repulsion limited to a few oversensitive members of naive, isolated, up-country native groups; the reaction has been widespread and is quite valid as one of the major **themes** of *No Longer at Ease*.

The Christian Science Monitor (January 26, 1966) has gone so far as to claim that the steadily growing "deepseated reaction to the massive corruption which undeniably existed in high places and which the government appeared to condone" was a determining factor in the military takeover and bloody purge that followed in 1966. In 1970, Labanji Bolaji published a study titled *Anatomy of Corruption in Nigeria* (Ibadan: Daystar Press). Writing about this subject in the *Nigerian Tribune* more recently, columnist Tai Solarin declares: "I have never noted bribery and corruption parading itself more shamefacedly and licentiously than it does today" (quoted in "Nigeria: The First Black Power," *Newsweek*, March 4, 1974, p. 13).

ACHEBE AS AFRICAN WRITER

Given this historical and sociological background, novelists throughout Africa and in Nigeria particularly have had no trouble fashioning tales. Unfortunately, most of the writing to date had been of a rather juvenile nature. Probably the best way to judge Achebe's achievements, and to fully appreciate his innovations and immense influence, is to read broadly in African literature, covering as large a time span and as many countries as possible.

By and large, the popular conception of African novels prior to *Things Fall Apart* bears little resemblance to Achebe's ground-breaking work. Nowhere, for example, is there a description of a lion hunt by a young man armed only with a spear and a leather shield, although such a hunt is alluded to in the novel. Still, *Things Fall Apart* is now considered the archetypal African novel, so much so that Charles R. Larson notes that in 1964 the book became "the first novel by an African writer to be included in the required syllabus for African secondary school students throughout the English-speaking portions of the continent" (*The Emergence of African Fiction*, rev. ed., Bloomington: Indiana University Press, 1972, p. 27).

PAN-AFRICAN PERSPECTIVE

To put Achebe in an African perspective, it would be helpful to read Olive Schreiner's 1883 novel, *The Story of an African Farm*; the work of South African Roy Campbell; Alan Paton's *Cry the Beloved Country* (1948); Kenyan James Ngugi (*The River Between*, 1965); and work from the Arabic north.

WEST AFRICAN PERSPECTIVE

To put Achebe in a West African perspective, the student might examine the novels of the first significant West African novelist, Ousamane Soce Diop (*Karim*, 1935, and *Mirages de Paris*, 1937) and his Senegalese compatriots, Abdoulaye Sadji (*Nini*, 1954), Cheikh Hemidou Kane (*L'aventur Ambique*, 1961), and Ousmane Semene (*O pays, mon beau peuple*, 1957), and of the Cameroonian, Mongo Beti (Le Pauvre Christ de Bomba, 1956). Senegal and Cameroon were the two areas most concerned with literature in the twentieth century prior to the emergence of Nigeria as a cultural leader. It would also be of value to study the work of writers from the Ivory Coast (Bernard Boua Dadie and Ake Loba), Ghana (Cameron Duodu's interesting *The Gab Boys*, 1967), Liberia (Bai T. Moore's *Murder in the Cassava Patch*, 1968, one of only two or three novels written by a Liberian), and Sierra Leone (novelist Abioseh Nicol and short story writer Eldred Durosimi Jones).

NIGERIAN PERSPECTIVE

To put Achebe in a Nigerian perspective, the student should first study the poets and playwrights of a generation ago: R. E. G. Armattoe, G. Adali-Mortty, J. H. Kwabena Nketia, I. Kafu Hoh,

A. K. Mensah, F. Parkes, G. Haga, H. K. B. Setsoafia, L. K. Idan, F. K. Fiawoo, J. B. Danquah, and M. Dei-Anang. Among the more current Nigerian writers are Wole Soyinka (the foremost African dramatist) and John Pepper Clark; poet Gabriel Okara; and novelists T. M. Aluko (*One Man, One Matchet*, 1964); Elechi Amadi (*The Concubine*, 1966); Cyprian Ekwensi (*Burning Grass*, 1962, and People of the City, 1954 - "the first modern Nigerian novel"); Nkem Nwankwo (*Danada*, 1964); Flora Nwapa (*Efuru*, 1966); and Onuora Nzekwu (*Wand of Noble Wood*, 1961).

ACHEBE'S INFLUENCE

More than any other novelist, Achebe has influenced his African contemporaries. Direct influences in terms of ideology, treatment of the past, and use of language can be traced in the works of James Ngugi, Vincent Ike (*Toads for Supper*, 1965), Elechi Amadi, and Flora Nwapa, among others. In the long run this influence on his fellow writers may be considered one of Achebe's most important accomplishments.

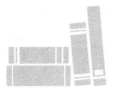

THINGS FALL APART

....

An author's Style is his characteristic manner of expression. There are many elements that combine to create an author's style, but style is basically determined by one thing; the writer's purpose. In speaking of a novelist's purpose, one includes not only the **theme** that the novelist is trying to express but also the effect that he wishes to impose upon his audience in relation to his theme.

ACHEBE'S PURPOSE

Achebe has spoken widely on what he considers to be the role of a writer and, in particular, the responsibilities of an African writer, and his fiction reflects his critical theorizing. In discussing "The Role of the Writer in a New Nation," he states; "I believe that the writer should be concerned with the question of human values" (*Nigeria Magazine*, No. 81, June 1964, p. 160). As a novelist, then, he attempts to educate his readers, to expose them to "human values":

The writer cannot be excused from the task of re- education and re-generation that must be done. In fact he

should march right in front. For he is after all - as Ezekiel Mphahlele says in his African Image - the sensitive point in his community.

("The Novelist as Teacher," *New Statesman*, 29 January 1965, p. 162)

As a novelist in a new nation, Achebe assumes a special responsibility in regards to his educational function. In speaking at a conference in Leeds in 1964, he noted;

... it would be foolish to pretend that we have fully recovered from the traumatic effects of our first confrontation with Europe. Three or four weeks ago my wife who teaches English in a boy's school asked a pupil why he wrote about winter when he meant the harmattan. He said he would be laughed out of class if he did such a thing! Now, you wouldn't have thought, would you, that there was something shameful in your weather? But apparently we do. How can this great blasphemy be purged? I think it is part of my business as a writer to teach that boy that there is nothing disgraceful about the African weather, that the palm-tree is a fit subject for poetry.

(Quoted in *Commonwealth Literature*, ed. John Press, London; Heinemann, 1965, p. 204)

For Achebe, the task of educating his fellow Africans is a great challenge and duty;

It is inconceivable to me that a serious writer could stand aside from this debate or be indifferent to this argument which calls his full humanity in question. For me, at any rate there is a clear duty to make a statement. This is my answer to those who say that a writer should be writing about contemporary issues - about politics in 1964, about city life, about the last coup d'etat. Of course, these are all legitimate themes for the writer but as far as I am concerned the fundamental theme must first be disposed of. This theme - put quite simply - is that African people did not hear of culture for the first time from Europeans; that their societies were not mindless but frequently had a philosophy of great depth and value and beauty, that they had poetry and, above all, they had dignity. It is this dignity that many African people all but lost during the colonial period, and it is this that they must now regain. The worst thing that can happen to any people is the loss of their dignity and self-respect. The writer's duty is to help them regain it by showing them in human terms what happened to them, what they lost. There is a saying in Ibo that a man who can't tell where the rain began to beat him cannot know where he dried his body. The writer can tell the people where the rain began to beat them.

("The Role of the Writer in a New Nation," p. 158)

Continuing his discussion of how the writer must educate, Achebe comments; "One of the most distressing ills which afflict new nations is a confusion of values. We sometimes make the mistake of talking about values as though they were fixed and eternal.... Of course values are relative and in a constant state of flux" ("The Role of the Writer in a New Nation," p. 159). "The writer in our society should be able to think of these things and bring them out in a form that is dramatic and memorable" ("The Role of the Writer in a New Nation," p. 160), Achebe asserts, and to do this he has turned to art; "Perhaps what I write is applied art as distinct from pure. But who cares? Art is important but so is education of the kind I have in mind" ("The Novelist as Teacher," p. 162).

Given his convictions about a writer's role, Achebe has similarly addressed himself to the question of how that role might best be carried out. As noted in the "Introduction," his prime requirement is honesty. The African writer "has a responsibility to avoid shoddiness in his work," he wrote in "The Role of the Writer in a New Nation" (p. 169). Observing that African writing has become popular, he adds that that very popularity might contain a danger in that it can tempt contemporary writers to do less than their best because they know that anything that they write will sell on the current market. One can do several things at once and still maintain a sense of integrity, Achebe realizes;

I would be quite satisfied if my novels ... did no more than teach my readers that their past - with all its imperfections - was not one long night of savagery from which the first Europeans acting on God's behalf delivered them ... and I don't see that [art and this didactic function] need be mutually exclusive.

(*Commonwealth Literature*, p. 205)

Elsewhere the novelist continues;

The question is how does a writer re-create this past? Quite clearly there is a strong temptation to select only those facts that will flatter him. If he succumbs he will have branded himself as an untrustworthy witness. But it is not only his personal integrity as an artist which is involved. The credibility of the world he is attempting to recreate will be called to question and he will defeat his own purpose if he is suspected of glossing over inconvenient facts. We cannot pretend that our past was one long, technicolour idyll. We have to admit that like other people's past ours had its good as well as its bad sides.

("The Role of the Writer in a New Nation," p. 158)

There is no doubt that Achebe has followed his own strictures in composing *Things Fall Apart.*

ACHEBE'S VILLAGE BACKGROUND

"My world - the one that interests me more than any other," Achebe is quoted as saying in Jonathan Cott's *Pipers at the Gates of Dawn; The Wisdom of Children's Literature* (New York; Random House, 1981), "is the world of the village. It is one, not the only, reality, but it is the one that the Ibo, who are my people, have preferred to all others." This influence is clear in the physical descriptions in *Things Fall Apart*, and in the descriptions of daily life and the essence of the people and the clan. It shaped the author, and it is his subject matter. Actually, Form and Function cannot be separated in literature, for what a writer says is to some extent determined by the format in which it is said. Just as the format depends upon what is being said, so Achebe's village legacy appears in his style too. For example, folktales and proverbs are an integral part of the writer's style, and these elements are obvious extensions of the influence in his life of the village of Ogidi, where he grew up. As a child, he was told folktales by his mother and older sister, a custom that is repeated by the characters in his novel. The practice is more than simply a means of drawing a picture of village life, however, it is a literary technique that is characteristic of his work. Bernth Lindfors has pointed out how important proverbs are in supporting, emphasizing, and even expressing Achebe's meaning; "... proverbs can serve as keys to an understanding of his novels because he uses them not merely to add touches of local color but to sound and reiterate themes, to sharpen characterization, to clarify conflict, and to focus on the values of the society he is portraying" ("The Palm-Oil with Which Achebe's Words Are Eaten," *African Literature Today*, No. 1, 1968). For Achebe, the village is the underlying thematic concept, the tune, and the instrument upon which the tune is played.

THE CONCEPT OF CHI

Chi is the personal god of Achebe's people. The importance of this concept is mirrored in the names of the Ibo people by virtue of the use of the word as a prefix in many of their names. The author's first name, Chinua, is a "shortened form of an expression that means 'May a chi fight for me,'" he has explained (quoted in *Something About the Author*, vol. 40, p. 23). He goes on to say that since the word refers to the "individual spirit," it is found in many combinations; his wife's name, Chinwe, means "Chi owns me"; his son's name, Chidi, translates as "Chi is here"; his daughter took the name Chioma, "Good chi."

Two scholarly studies have been devoted to examining the concept of chi; Donatus Nwoga's "The Chi Offended," in *Transition* (Vol. IV, no. 15[1964], p. 5), and Austin J. Shelton's "The Offended Chi in Achebe's Novels," also in *Transition* (No. 13, 1964).

OVERALL STYLE

Abiola Irele sums up Achebe's methods and achievement in "The Tragic Conflict in Achebe's Novels," an article that appeared in *Black Orpheus* (No. 17, 1965), when he says (p. 32):

He is concerned primarily with individuals. His narrative method is detached, almost impassive, made of objective formulations through which the human drama is unfolded.

Yet it is not impersonal, for instead of flamboyant colours of a heated imagination, we have rather the clear lines that compose a picture by a dispassionate observer of human destiny, who constructs a vision out of his awareness of an inexorable order. Achebe has justly been called a chronicler, for in the last resort, he is not dealing with the collapse of the African Society, but with its transformation. He is examining from the inside the historical evolution of the African Society at its moments of crisis, and the inevitable tensions attendant upon this process. In the final analysis, his novels reveal the intimate circumstances of the African Becoming.

LANGUAGE

Achebe's most important technical device is probably his use of language, not only in the traditional sense of **imagery**, symbolism, and so forth (although these elements are present), but also in his utilization of several different dialects of English. Even though the use of English dialects is not an important factor in *Things Fall Apart*, the use of the English language itself as a medium of expression has been one of his major concerns. Indeed, 9e has felt compelled at times to justify his writing in English, as when he said; "There are not many countries in Africa today where you could abolish the language of the erstwhile colonial powers and still retain the facility for mutual communication. Therefore those African writers who have chosen to write in English or French are not unpatriotic smart alecks with an eye on the main chance - outside their own countries. They are by-products of the same processes that made the new nation states of Africa" ("The English Language and the African Writer," *Transition*, No. 18, 1965, rpt. Insight, October/ December 1966, pp. 19–20). "I have been given this language and I intend to use it," he concludes. Since Achebe has openly stated that his primary reason for writing is to educate, and since the modern literary **theme** of communication (or the lack of it) is one of his fundamental interests, his advocacy of English as the best medium for expressing himself seems valid in this context.

"The African writer," he goes on to say, "should aim to use English in a way that brings out his message best without altering the language to the extent that its value as a medium of international exchange will be lost. He should aim at fashioning out an English which is at once universal and able to carry his peculiar experience." The novelist insists, though, that English, or any language for that matter, must be used correctly;

... my answer to the question, Can an African ever learn English well enough to be able to use it effectively in creative writing? is certainly yes. If on the other hand you ask: Can he ever learn to use it as a native speaker? I should say: I hope not. It is neither necessary nor desirable for him to be able to do so.

("The English Language and the African Writer," p. 21)

Furthermore, Achebe is of the opinion that a serious writer must use that language which is powerful enough to contain and express his message - "an animal whose blood can match the power of his offering," as he puts it. Possibly this is why he employs a Biblical phrasing in much of *Things Fall Apart*. Such power contains dangers, too, of course:

For an African, writing in English is not without its serious set-backs. He often finds himself describing situations or modes of thought which have no direct equivalent in the English way of life. Caught in that situation he can do one of two things. He can try and contain what

20

he wants to say within the limit of conventional English or he can try to push back those limits to accommodate his ideas. The first method produces competent, uninspired and rather flat work. The second method can produce something new and valuable to the English language as well as to the material he is trying to put over. But it can also get out of hand. It can lead to bad English being accepted and defended as African or Nigerian. I submit that those who can do the work of extending the frontiers of English so as to accommodate African thought-patterns must do it through their mastery of English and not out of innocence.

("The Role of the Writer in a New Nation," p. 160)

In discussing Achebe's linguistic qualities, Gerald Moore contends;

Achebe needed an English vocabulary of images, allusions and metaphors utterly new to the novel, yet he was able to discover these simply by fidelity to the way men and women still spoke in the quieter villages of his own childhood. A judicious mixture of translation and authentic invention produced a conversational style which walked through his pages with all the weight of formality, precedence and tradition, yet never stumbled over itself through ineptitude.

(*The Chosen Tongue*, London; Longmans, 1969, p. 152)

REASONING IN IMAGES

Eldred Jones, speaking of Achebe's use of language, has caught the essence of its effect;

... he required a medium which would be universally accessible, but which would also ring true in the mouths of characters whose outlook and ideas were very different from those usually conveyed by English. He therefore loaded English with freight from the traditional Ibo mind and, without changing the structure of the language, changed its character. Anyone reading Achebe is conscious that the language has a basic inspiration independent of English: His characters reason in images rather than words, and there is a pleasing non-Englishness in their speech.

("Jungle Drums and Wailing Piano," *African Forum*, Vol. 1, No. 4, 1966, p. 96)

IBO WORDS AND PROVERBS

Achebe spices his narrative with bits of Ibo. At times this seems to be an affectation. On the other hand, there is no doubt that this practice provides some of the flavor of the milieu that he is attempting to recreate, and the importance that the author attaches to this practice is demonstrated by the glossary of Ibo words that he includes at the end of the book.

Achebe's use of proverbs is of a piece with his occasional use of an Ibo vocabulary. As the narrator says in the very first chapter of the novel, "Among the Ibo the art of conversation is regarded very highly, and proverbs are the palm-oil with which words are eaten." The proverbs are incorporated in the story naturally, as they would be in the oral tradition that they are drawn from and that they simultaneously exemplify.

All in all, then, language is a major element of Achebe's technical arsenal, not only for creating an African atmosphere, but also for characterization and for stressing his themes. The narrative of *Things Fall Apart*, with its sprinkling of Ibo words and expressions, gives a feeling of strength and maturity; the narrative of *No Longer at Ease*, with its different levels of English usage, gives a feeling of youth. To some extent the difference is established by the harsher, simpler vocabulary and sentence structure of the earlier novel, but it also grows out of the more effete consciousness of the subtle differences between the languages shared by Obi and his friends. In *Things Fall Apart* language is considered powerful in itself and used accordingly, whereas *No Longer at Ease* concentrates on concepts and subtleties, and the language reflects this focus. It is the difference between primal action and civilized talk; between instinctive reaction and tempered, considered conciliation; between the broadsword and the foil, or, more appropriately, between the machete and the pen.

THIRD-PERSON NARRATOR

Since Achebe's narrator employs Ibo words and uses proverbial material, since he fills his tale with details of daily life in the village and in the culture, it is interesting that the narration is done in the third person. This technique allows for an Omniscient Observer. An omniscient observer is one who knows everything, as opposed to a first-person narrator who can speak only from his or her own immediate point of view. While there may be some diminishment of emotional content, the use of an omniscient observer permits the author to present his material with more authority for he is not speaking for himself; instead he is merely reporting what he sees. It also allows Achebe to present several different points of view on an equal basis and to incorporate details that he could not have included if the narrator were Okonkwo, who would have been limited in his narration to those things that he knew or saw himself. Thus, opinions, beliefs, and emotions of other villagers and the white men are brought to the reader's attention.

ADDITIONAL TECHNIQUES

Achebe frequently relies on other devices in order to express himself. He constantly uses repetition - of ideas, words and phrases, parables, and images. He juxtaposes appearance and reality during the entire course of the novel, using contrasting descriptions as in the depictions of Okonkwo's apparent reaction to the priestess's carrying off Ezinma in one chapter and his actual reaction in later pages.

The novel is filled with **irony** and symbolism, with the figure of Okonkwo being the most obvious example as he represents his clan's traditional culture, and also as seen in the affair of the killing of the sacred python. Achebe even uses literary **allusions** (references to Yeats being the paramount example of this technique) and the examples that he draws upon reinforce his subtle use of language in this story. He also includes a great many folk elements-tales and legends and especially the parables, which at times are used as **imagery**. Finally, as Albert Gerard has pointed out, Achebe's work is a "serious social and psychological analysis," and his interest is concentrated on the individual. Aside from the **protagonist**, the majority of his characters are not fully drawn (the women in particular). Nevertheless, they give a realistic impression because of the little humanizing touches which he adds (as seen in Ekwefi's constant concern for Ezinma, the exchanges between the mother and daughter about whether fire burns adults while they are preparing dinner, and the descriptions of Okonkwo's wives' huts and cooking habits). Their motivations and reactions are understandable; their thoughts are easy to follow (even those of Mr. Smith - Achebe does not portray him, or any other white man, as a complete ogre), giving us a basis for comprehending what is happening and why, instead of being faced with mere stereotypes. This increases the author's credibility, naturally, and relates to his desire to present things as they are rather than in polemic blindness. Much of Achebe's technique can be seen as having been derived from the African oral tradition. The simple, repetitive qualities of the novel surely stem from this base.

QUOTIDIAN DETAILS

As has been amply noted throughout this study, one of Achebe's major stylistic characteristics is his careful and exhaustive detailing of the minutiae of village life - the use of palm-wine, cowrie shells as a medium of exchange, bamboo beds, the town crier, palm-oil lamps, the cooking habits of the women. This provides a realistic background for the action and helps place the **protagonist** in his culture.

In addition, Achebe depicts the clan's traditions, such as ritualistic prayer to the ancestors for life and health in Chapter One and the bargaining for a bride in Chapter Eight. These seemingly incidental details help confirm the importance of established religion in the life of the clan and of Okonkwo.

CONTRAST

Related to and an outgrowth of the detailing of the clan's everyday life and beliefs is the novelist's frequent use of contrast. The plot line, for instance, introduces Chielo, the priestess of Agbala, as an ordinary, friendly, caring woman, in contrast to her personality when she decrees Ikemefuna's fate. The purpose of such a contrast is to demonstrate the differentiation between the human being and the abstract concepts that bind the clan together.

THINGS FALL APART

On another level, contrast is utilized not just to reinforce a **theme** but to actually express it. This is evident in the overall structure of *Things Fall Apart*. The novel is divided into three sections:

Part One (Chapters One through Thirteen). In Part One, Achebe presents a picture of village life over a period of thirty to forty years.

Part Two (Chapters Fourteen through Nineteen). Okonkwo's seven-year-exile is portrayed in this section.

Part Three (Chapters Twenty through Twenty-five). The final section depicts Okonkwo's return to Umuofiai, his confrontation with the white man's ways, and his suicide.

The concept of contrast is illustrated in this structure, for Achebe needed to spend a considerable amount of time drawing a picture of the culture that encompasses Okonkwo in order for us to understand it and to have a benchmark against which to measure the changes that take place during the course of the novel, particularly those related to the intrusion of the white man.

The total effect of Achebe's style is a novel obviously written by one with great familiarity with English literature and a facility in the use of the English language, but one who is also at home with the traditions, languages, and conditions of Nigeria - which is exactly what *Things Fall Apart* is all about.

THINGS FALL APART

CHAPTER ONE

. . . .

Things Fall Apart opens with a description of Okonkwo, the protagonist, which depicts his character, his history, and his physical attributes.

Protagonist comes from the Greek meaning "first combatant." The term is applied to the central, principal leading character of a literary work and should be distinguished from Hero, which involves heroic (noble, courageous) action and, according to Aristotle, sufficient status to make his fall noticeable and important to society as a whole. (Aristotle was a fourth-century B.C. Greek philosopher and critic who defined the nature of classical tragic drama.) In this case, the main character certainly embodies heroic characteristics, for Okonkwo is a warrior-leader who exhibits "special strength, ability, and courage" (see Harry Shaw, *Concise Dictionary of Literary Terms*, New York: McGraw-Hill, 1976). Indeed, Okonkwo demonstrates many of the elements attributed to Aristotelian tragic

heroes. Among these is hamartia, the tragic flaw, which will be discussed below.

Part of the value and appeal of this novel lies in Achebe's detailing of the everyday life of the nine villages, and in particular of Umuofia, in what would become the nation of Nigeria, in the days immediately before the coming of the white man. The traditions, the foods, the tools and weapons, the songs and stories, the clothing, the daily activities all serve as a background to the action in *Things Fall Apart*; but these details are simultaneously an important part of the story that Achebe is telling, for he must establish a benchmark against which changes can be measured, and he must also portray Okonkwo's world in such a way that we can understand the nature of the man by understanding his environment and background. Thus, when we learn about Okonkwo's skill as a wrestler, we are being instructed about tribal values and traditions at the same time that our portrait of Okonkwo is being fleshed out.

Along these lines, in describing the feat of Okonkwo's defeating the master wrestler called the Cat, Achebe both characterizes his **protagonist** and establishes in a natural way the importance of the tribal elders as a repository of knowledge and information. Here, for instance, the clan's history is introduced in a mythic form in the tale of the town's father who fought a spirit for seven days and nights. This information about the village's history and traditions is vital to comprehending Okonkwo's makeup, probably even more significant to an understanding of the novel than the facts that the wrestling match took place more than twenty years ago and that Okonkwo's fame has continued to grow since that time.

If Okonkwo is seen as an Aristotelian hero, the facts that he is famous and physically imposing serve to demonstrate that he is of sufficient stature to capture our attention, but more critical is the revelation that he has no patience with failure and that he tends to resort to physical violence when he is angered. These traits foreshadow the course of his life and are reflected in his name, which means "The Roaring Flame."

Foreshadowing is the indicating of or hinting at events that will transpire later. Over the length of the work these suggestions accumulate to give an added depth to the work, helping the author develop an atmosphere which carries part of his meaning, even at a subconscious level.

OKONKWO'S FATHER

Okonkwo's impatience with weakness and his propensity for violence derive from his relationship with his father, Unoka. Unoka has been dead for ten years when the novel opens, yet his influence on Okonkwo is profound. In contrast to his son, Unoka was tall and thin, lazy, improvident, "incapable of thinking about tomorrow," a palm-wine drunkard, and a very good flute player. This last shows an interest in things artistic, a trait that Okonkwo equates with weakness and femininity; much of what motivates Okonkwo is related to his definition of gender roles - he is proud of being a man and embarrassed whenever "feminine" attributes or actions surface. The fun-loving, carefree nature of the father is antithetical to the staid, focused son.

THE CONCEPT OF HAMARTIA, THE FATAL FLAW

The portrayal of Unoka provides for a contrast with Okonkwo, helping to develop the image of the **protagonist** in the reader's mind. At the same time, knowing how Okonkwo feels about his father's failures and his fear that he might also fail supplies the primary ingredients needed to understand the son's motivation. It is this aspect of Okonkwo's nature that constitutes his Aristotelian tragic flaw.

Hamartia, or the tragic flaw, is a literary concept expounded by Aristotle. Since the heroes in classical tragedy were so outstanding, it would have been considered inappropriate for them to suffer at the hands of the gods. Therefore, an explanation had to be devised that would allow for their destruction. Hamartia is that explanation. Derived from the Greek word for "fault," according to this concept, there is a deadly flaw in the protagonist that leads to his deserved downfall. This weakness in an otherwise admirable and undefeatable character often takes the form of ignorance or an overweening pride.

Okonkwo's tragic flaw is his fear of personal weakness and failure. Everything that he does is colored by this fear and determines how he will react in any situation; ultimately, Okonkwo's hamartia will lead to his death.

Incidentally, some critics, such as Charles R. Larson, claim that it is not valid to comment on the Aristotelian elements in this novel, since the story is about Africa and not about a Western **protagonist**; these critics apparently overlook the fact that Achebe was educated in a system that would have exposed him to Aristotelian concepts and patterns, so whether or not he consciously included such elements is unimportant - they are clearly there. Moreover, the fact that the novelist drew on Western author William Butler Yeats for the source of his novel's title (see the discussion of this important feature below) would seem to belie the contention that such ingredients are neither intended not applicable.

OKONKWO'S ACHIEVEMENTS

A further contrast used to develop Okonkwo's character, following the extended description of his father is a chapter-concluding summary of his achievements up to this point in his life.

FORESHADOWING

It is ironic that Okonkwo's strength of character develops from his father's weakness of character. It is also ironic that the source of his strength is at the same time the source of his weakness and finally of his downfall and death.

Irony is a figure of speech in which the intended meaning is the opposite of that expressed. Irony exploits the difference between Appearance And Reality, and as such it is the very stuff of artistic literature. *Things Fall Apart* abounds with ironies which will be pointed out during the course of this examination.

THINGS FALL APART

CHAPTER TWO

....

In Chapter Two, there is a shift in tense; the narration of the story begins when the sound of drums passes a message through the night calling ten thousand men of the tribe to a meeting in the marketplace the next morning. The picture of the night that the author paints contains items that underscore the superstitious nature of the clan and continues the delineation of the prosaic elements of daily life that contribute to the background out of which Okonkwo's character was molded.

INITIATING EVENTS

At the meeting, Ogbuefi Ezeugo announces the murder of Ogbuefi Udo's wife near the town of Mbaino. According to the clan's tradition, her death could be avenged either by the village going to war or by the guilty party's furnishing a young man and a virgin girl in compensation. The town's decision will have a profound effect on Okonkwo, for it will expose him and his family to the weaknesses that bedevil him.

INTRODUCTION OF THE ORACLE

The strength and history of Umuofia is recounted; the village is the holder of powerful "war-medicine," but the elders decide to offer terms to Mbaino. In describing these events, the narrator mentions the Oracle of the Hills and Caves for the first time. This connection is important for two reasons. One, it is made clear that the villagers do not act on important matters without consulting the Oracle and that the Oracle's advice is followed (there are times, we are informed, when the Oracle opposes warfare, and the village would never dare go to war without the Oracle's approval). The importance of tradition and the regard with which the tribe's leaders are held is thus established. Two, the importance of the Oracle and the tribe's obedience having been established, the interaction between Okonkwo's family and the Oracle is simultaneously prepared for. Since Okonkwo is such a strong supporter of the clan's mores, the ironies that will develop have been prepared for, and his acceptance of the Oracle's will coincidentally demonstrates an important facet of his character.

OKONKWO AS EMISSARY

Okonkwo's stature in the clan is evidenced by his being chosen to carry the village's terms for retribution to Mbaino.

IRONY AND OKONKWO'S CHARACTER

There is further delineation of the protagonist's nature as his temper and fear of failure and weakness are revealed in his treatment of his own family. A psychological explanation begins to evolve, for it is evident that he has a passionate fear that he will be like his father, leading him to hate gentleness and idleness, even in his own children, and particularly in his son, Nwoye. Ironically, Nwoye may not be nearly as effeminate as Okonkwo perceives him to be, and it may also be that Okonkwo's treatment of the twelve-year-old boy forces the youngster to fit the image that his father has created - another instance of **irony** as a self-fulfilling prophecy evolves. Against this psychological background the figures of Okonkwo's three wives and eight children and the description of his property and holdings seem a solid contrast, yet they are all really nothing more than evidence of what motivations drive the husband/father/farmer.

IKEMEFUNA

The young man who returns from Mbaino with Okonkwo as part of the reparation for Ogbuefi Udo's murdered wife is a lad of fifteen named Ikemefuna. It is decided that he will live with Okonkwo's family until the clan decides what to do with him, a decision that will be three years in coming. Again **irony** underscores the sequence of events. Ikemefuna becomes Nwoye's best friend, so when the hostage is killed, Nwoye will be especially affected by the rationale behind the murder. Moreover, Okonkwo sees the contrast between the two boys as they are engaged in household tasks and as they learn the actions that Okonkwo deems important in defining the character of a man. In Okonkwo's eyes the comparison only serves to make Nwoye appear more weak. Also, Ikemefuna becomes endeared to Okonkwo, more so than his own son is, so that Okonkwo's acceptance of and participation in Ikemefuna's murder is doubly ironic.

THINGS FALL APART

CHAPTER THREE

. . . .

Chapter Three opens with an illustration of the impact of the Oracle of the Hills and the Caves on the life of Okonkwo's family. Superficially and symbolically the law and wisdom of the clan reside in the Oracle, but there is another significance, too, for there is symbolism that revolves around the Oracle that touches Okonkwo directly. His obedience and acceptance of the Oracle's decisions symbolize his attachment to the fabric that defines the clan. The **irony** of this situation lies in how he suffers because of the Oracle. If he had no allegiance to the Oracle, if he did not believe in it unquestioningly, the outcome of his life would have been very different.

A symbol is something that stands for, is regarded as, or represents something else. It is a material or physical thing that suggests something larger than itself, often something that is nonmaterial or psychological. Money, for instance, is symbolic of labor, and the stars and stripes on the American flag symbolize the states and the original colonies that

comprise the United States. Symbolism is the use of symbols in a structured way to supply a symbolic character and/or meaning to something. Thus, Okonkwo's association of the Oracle with the spiritual and legal constitution of his clan's essence embodies the elements that constitute his nature as well, and his acquiescence to the Oracle comes to stand for those specific aspects of his makeup.

UNOKA

The tale of Okonkwo's visit to the Oracle in the company of his father, Unoka, is particularly significant because of Okonkwo's attitude toward the Oracle, who blames Unoka's problems on laziness. This would reaffirm Okonkwo's feelings about his father and his father's weaknesses. When Unoka dies from a swelling of the stomach and limbs and therefore cannot be buried because his body would be an abomination to the earth goddess, it must have seemed to the young Okonkwo that such a death was a just dessert for his father's life. The nature of Unoka's dying, then, confirms Okonkwo's worst fears.

CHI

At this point, the concept of the chi is introduced. Given his father's history and the state of Unoka's property, Okonkwo's start in life was considered depressed. It is from this base, naturally, that his achievements will be measured, and although he did not have a prosperous start in life, Okonkwo strove, slowly and painfully, to overcome his disadvantaged heritage. The fact that the successful farmer Nwakibie is willing to provide Okonkwo with eight hundred yams, twice what he hoped for, so that the young man can become a sharecropper is proof that

Okonkwo's spirit and hard work are recognized by others. At the same time, this largesse is also seen as evidence that Okonkwo's chi is a good one. A chi is a personal god that controls one's destiny, so this concept is extremely important in the life of the individual clanspeople. (It is of no little consequence that yams are symbolic of masculinity in Okonkwo's society.)

SEEDS ARE SOWN

More is learned about Okonkwo's earlier years. Because of his father's inability to support the family, the son took on the responsibility of providing for his mother, father, and two sisters, an admirable accomplishment. In suffering through the drought year, after having obtained the yam seed from Nwakibie, Okonkwo is marked by an inflexible will to survive. His father's words, meant to hearten him during the worst drought in living memory, are irony-laden and have the tone of Greek tragedy about them. When Unoka says, "Do not despair.... A proud heart can survive a general failure because such a failure does not prick its pride. It is more difficult and more bitter when a man fails alone," he is describing his own fate. Likewise, Unoka is putting his finger on his son's nature, for Okonkwo is a proud man who will not tolerate failure. Okonkwo's reaction is realistic; he has no patience with the dying man or his words. Still, when the end comes for Okonkwo, it comes because he is unable to accept the general failure of his clan in the face of the white man's society.

THINGS FALL APART

CHAPTER FOUR

. . . .

OKONKWO'S RELATIONSHIPS WITH OTHERS

Okonkwo's character is further elucidated in Chapter Four, as his rapid rise from great poverty to a position as one of the lords of the clan is detailed. In spite of his success, however, he is not sympathetic towards those whom he considers weak - or effeminate, as he defines the trait. An example of this attitude is found in his brusque treatment of Osugo, whom he calls a woman when the other man contradicts him in a meeting. That Okonkwo is overreacting is demonstrated by the reactions of the other men at the meeting, who chastise him for his words and call him fortunate.

Okonkwo apologizes, but the narrator states that Okonkwo was not helped by a benevolent spirit; rather he helped himself and deserved his success. Still, his chi must have been good. The inference that can be made here is that the chi is somehow a combination, being both a personal god and a reflection of the inner man.

IKEMEFUNA AND NWOYE

Okonkwo's relationship with Ikemefuna is further delineated in this chapter, particularly as it contrasts with his relationship with Nwoye. The relationship between the two boys is also detailed - they become inseparable and Ikemefuna functions as Nwoye's older brother.

THEMATIC EVOLUTIONS

By interweaving characters and plot elements throughout his story, as in the case of Ikemefuna and Nwoye, Achebe is starting to develop the **themes** of the novel.

Plot is the arranged order of events as the narrator chooses to divulge them. Notice that it differs, therefore, from Story, which is the actual chronological order of those events. A Theme is a central and dominant idea, usually determining the author's methods of expression since it is the implicit message carried by the plot.

OJIUGO

Okonkwo is angered when Ojiugo, his youngest wife, is not home to cook his afternoon meal. He beats her, forgetting that the clan is celebrating the Week of Peace, a time when physical violence is forbidden. Ezeani, a priest of Ani, the earth goddess, demands a sacrifice of a she-goat, a hen, a length of cloth, and one hundred cowries as the price for Okonkwo's redemption.

THEMES MANIFEST

This is an important event in the narrative, for while Okonkwo is inwardly repentant for his action, he does not demonstrate his feelings outwardly, since he feels that to do so would be a sign of weakness. The result is that the people in the village believe that he has no respect for the gods. The **themes** manifest in this sequence of actions are: (1) Okonkwo's uncontrollable anger and physical reaction to situations in which his anger is stimulated (which will be the proximate cause of his death); (2) his power to run the household, which is part of the background of Ibo tradition that defines the man and his culture; (3) the power of tradition that subdues him and that allows him to accept his punishment for a transgression even though he is not convinced that what he did was totally wrong, given the circumstances which triggered his outburst; and (4) the ever-present fear of weakness and the appearance of weakness that governs his every action. The fact that Okonkwo's religious offense is the main topic of conversation in the village is a further demonstration of how important tradition is in the Ibo culture.

PLANTING TIME

There follows a description of the activities involved in planting yams, another of the many particulars of Nigerian daily life that Achebe presents in order to build a picture of Okonkwo's culture.

THINGS FALL APART

CHAPTER FIVE

....

FEAST OF THE NEW YAM

The detailing of events surrounding the central place of the yam in Ibo village life is continued as the narrator explains the festival of the Feast of the New Yam. This involves some discussion of Ani, the earth goddess who is the source of fertility. Ani is also the ultimate judge of morality and conduct for the clan, for she is in communion with the clan's forefathers. The Feast of the New Yam is held before the harvest and is used to dispose of the past year's yams in honor of Ani and the clan's ancestral spirits. Despite the traditional basis for the ceremony, Okonkwo does not like feasts; he would rather work.

EKWEFI

Another incident involving Okonkwo's wrath occurs when Ekwefi, his second wife, cuts a banana tree, and he shoots at her, much to the amusement of the villagers. Again it is demonstrated that Okonkwo has a violent temper - and that his temper is a symptom of what pushes him to succeed. At the same time, the description of an everyday domestic scene, cooking, reveals some of the softness that underlies and is overcome by his fears. It is sad that at the base it appears that Okonkwo would be content to be a loving husband, father, and provider, but he is driven by personal demons that effectively blunt any tender impulses that he might have. The juxtaposition of Okonkwo's tempestuous outbursts and the domestic tranquility is part of a sequence of scenes that in the aggregate explain how he can be so callous when it comes time to obey the Oracle and kill Ikemefuna.

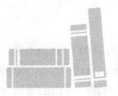

THINGS FALL APART

CHAPTER SIX

. . . .

WRESTLING CONTEST

Most of this chapter is taken up by a description and explanation of the wrestling contest. This is an important event in the tribe's daily life for it helps establish who the new rulers will be by reinforcing the concept of masculinity, the prime component of leadership, as defined by physical strength.

INTIMATIONS OF THINGS TO COME?

Maduka wins the match with the first use of a new move. Ironically, this new move may actually be a boxing blow imported by invading white men - which would be the first and a literal example of the overthrowing of Ibo customs by white customs. If this is so, there is a double **irony** in that Okonkwo is especially full of praise for the young man's demonstration of prowess.

EZINMA

Ekwefi talks with Chielo, a priestess of Agbala, about her daughter Ezinma - who is likely to have "come to stay" because she is now ten years old (most Ibo children died before the age of six). Chielo is presented as an ordinary, caring, and friendly woman.

IBO MENTALITY

As will be seen later, Chielo is not always so humane, and the difference between her treatment of Ezinma and Ikemefuna sums up a vital difference between the Ibo and Christian religions. When she is in the role of priestess, her concerns are clan-oriented to the extent that she is incapable of allowing her personality to rule her decisions. Whatever is determined to be best for the clan, even if this is a demand for the death of an innocent being, is paramount and unquestioned. It is this attitude that will drive Nwoye away from his heritage and into the more gentle Christian camp.

A COMMON EXPERIENCE

Chielo's introduction comes against the backdrop of the villagers' common experience of the wrestling match and the shared communal spirit that is evoked and emotionally reinforced by the rhythmic drumming. In this way, Achebe is also demonstrating that the dichotomy in her nature is an acceptable part of the clan's view of life.

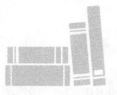

THINGS FALL APART

CHAPTER SEVEN

....

IKEMEFUNA'S ADJUSTMENT

Ikemefuna has become a member of the family at this point, and he is a good influence on Nwoye, helping the younger boy to mature.

NWOYE'S PREFERENCES

In a bit of **foreshadowing**, we see that Nwoye prefers his mother's folktales to his father's masculine stories of tribal wars full of violence and bloodshed and headhunting.

LOCUSTS

The coming of the locusts is part of the natural course of life for the clan. The locusts are also an indication that death is part of life. This, together with the details of how the locusts are consumed, might be offensive to a Western audience, much as the subsequent events are.

DEATH DECREE

Ezeuda comes to tell Okonkwo that after three years the Oracle of the Hills has decided that Ikemefuna must be killed. In making this announcement, Ezeuda says that "Umuofia has decided," an illustration of how the Oracle speaks for, is representative of, the village. Although the decision has been a long time in the making, it must be remembered that Ikemefuna was taken in retribution for the murder of Udo's wife. Okonkwo is warned that he should not participate in Ikemefuna's death because the young man calls him "father."

THE MURDER

In spite of the warning not to participate, when Ikemefuna is taken into the forest by the men, it is Okonkwo who delivers the death blow to Ikemefuna. Okonkwo commits this act out of fear of being thought weak. It is perhaps a self-damning act as well, one from which Okonkwo who will never fully recover, one which foreshadows the death of the head messenger in Chapter Twenty-Four, and one which justifies Okonkwo's eventual death at his own hands.

NWOYE'S REACTION

In another piece of **foreshadowing** that emanates from this event, Nwoye's reaction is related; he remembers how upset he was previously when he realized the inhumanity of some of the clan's practices, epitomized by the tribal custom of disposing of newborn twin babies by abandoning them in the bush. These events will come to Nwoye's mind again when he hears the empathetic messages of the Christians. The contrast between his father's beliefs and actions and those taught by the Christian church ultimately bring about the destruction of the family unit, an overwhelming burden on Okonkwo.

THINGS FALL APART

OKONKWO'S REMORSE AND GUILT

For several days after Ikemefuna's killing, Okonkwo is so beset by remorse that he mopes around his obi, the large quarters where the head of the family lives. Finally, he decides to visit his best friend, Obierika. At Obierika's Okonkwo meets Maduka, Obierika's son and the winner of the wrestling match.

During the conversation, it is clear that Obierika recognizes that his friend has made a mistake in taking part in Ikemefuna's murder and that what he did will not please the Earth: "It is the kind of action for which the goddess wipes out whole families," he notes. There is an obvious contrast between how the fathers treat their sons and the degree of their sons' successes, somewhat along the lines sketched by Arthur Miller in *Death of a Salesman* when Willy Loman sees how his sons have turned out (they are failures) in comparison with his neighbor's son (a successful attorney). Okonkwo's refusal to be thought weak, and his resulting participation in the murder, is again equated with the concept of the tragic flaw of Greek drama.

STORY OF NDULUE

Ofoedu comes in at this point and tells the men about the death of the strong man and former battle leader Ogbuefi Ndulue of Ire village. The drum has not yet been beaten for his death because his wife, Ozoemina, subsequently died and has to be buried first. Okonkwo finds it hard to believe that one who has been so strong in his youth could have had "one mind" with his wife to the extent that she would die immediately after he expired. Perhaps the insertion of this tale here is meant to parallel Okonkwo's story, for what he perceives as weakness in Ndulue is the same emotion that is gripping him now - the strength of the link between two people who love each other.

BRIDE BARTER

A group of men visit Obierika for the purpose of bargaining for his daughter, Akueke, to be a bride for Ibe. This activity and the rites and ceremonies attendant to it stress the traditions and established procedures of the clan while at the same time demonstrating that even in the midst of tragedy, life goes on (a sentiment eloquently expressed in W. H. Auden's "Musee des Beaux Artes," a modern poem that Achebe must be familiar with, since it comes from the same period as W.B. Yeat's poetry).

ENTER THE WHITE MAN

For the first time in the novel the existence of white men is mentioned, jokingly, in connection with leprosy. Leprosy is an infectious disease of the tropics and subtropics that can involve anesthesia, paralysis, and gangrene in the limbs, ears, and nose (which causes those members to fall off), among other symptoms. It flourishes in filth and squalor, and because it is so horrible, sufferers are frequently banished so that they will not infect others. Because the patient's skin turns white as the disease advances, the relating of Europeans to lepers is a natural, logical progression, though the symbolism of this joining of the disease and the invaders goes beyond the color of their skins - as leprosy destroys the individual's body, so will the white men destroy Okonkwo's civilization, lopping off vital parts piece by piece. Another ironic element is introduced later (in Chapter Eighteen) when the Christians' treatment of lepers, which is counter to the clan's tradition, stirs up a controversy.

THINGS FALL APART

CHAPTER NINE

HUMANIZING EFFECT OF EZINMA'S FEVER

Carrying over the concept of illness and disease into Chapter Nine, the narrator describes Ezinma's bout with iba (fever). The concern that her parents have for her is the common, universal feeling that parents have when their children are sick. This incident provides for the further humanizing of the characters, much as happens in Mark Twain's *Adventures of Huckleberry Finn* when Huck and Jim are on the raft and Jim recounts the tale of his mistreatment of his daughter because he did not realize that she was deaf. Jim suddenly becomes human in Huck's eyes when he understands the man's human qualities, and readers become more sensitive to the characters in Achebe's novel when they see the pain that Ezinma's parents share.

OGBANJE CHILDREN

In fleshing out the figures in his story, Achebe introduces the concept of ogbanje children, those who are bad, who die young, and who are born over and over again in a desperate cycle. Okabue, the medicine man, conducts a search for Ezinma's iyi-uwa, a symbolic rock. When discovered, this rock can be dealt with so that Ezinma's bondage in the ogbanje cycle can be broken.

OKONKWO'S MEDICINE

The chapter ends with Okonkwo demonstrating his love for his child, and his knowledge, by gathering leaves, grasses, and tree bark to make medicine that will cure his daughter. Although Achebe does not follow through and show Ezinma getting better, at the conclusion of the chapter it is indicated that her fever is breaking, and when the girl is next seen, she has recovered.

THINGS FALL APART

CHAPTER TEN

. . . .

EGWUGWU

This chapter is devoted to an explanation and illustration of the concept of egwugwu in the clan's religious beliefs. Egwugwu are the symbolic masqueraders who impersonate ancestral spirits. Actually, they are the male leaders of the tribe dressed in costume; while they are in costume the men become the spirits whom they are impersonating-Okonkwo's family does not "recognize" him when he is in this guise.

An important segment of tribal life is epitomized by the egwugwu, for not only do they embody the clan's beliefs, they also serve as arbiters of the villagers' actions. In this case they literally act as judges in a trial regarding a wife who ran away because her husband beat her. The acceptance of the egwugwu's decisions, that is to say, the decisions of the tribal leaders which are based on a body of tradition, is thereby once again made manifest.

THINGS FALL APART

CHAPTER ELEVEN

| EKWEFI

Achebe alternates the detailing of tribal life and lore with the characterizing of his main figures. In Chapter Ten he began the process of humanizing Ekwefi when he showed her concern for her sick daughter. In Chapter Eleven he continues this process by revealing more human touches about her, creating a person who is recognizable and to whom the reader can relate. In her function as an educator of her child, Ekwefi tells a folktale about Tortoise, traditionally an intelligent and cunning character in African folklore. The mythical explanation for why Tortoise's shell is not smooth may represent how words can lead the innocent and naive astray, much as the Christian missionaries will do later. That Tortoise pays for his deceit is not so important a point as that he tricks his victims rather easily.

CHIELO AND EZINMA

Chielo, the priestess of Agbala, comes to Okonkwo's compound and takes Ezinma away. Throughout the night Ekwefi follows them to the clan's farthest village and then back to Agbala's cave, even though she knows that she should leave the fate of her daughter up to the priestess. While she waits outside the cave, Okonkwo joins her. Although it seems at first glance that he does not care as much about his daughter as his wife does, he does appear. His feelings will be expanded upon in the next chapter.

THINGS FALL APART

CHAPTER TWELVE

. . . .

SUSPENSE

Chapter Twelve does not immediately continue with the narrative of Ezinma's night with Chielo. Instead, suspense is created as the narrator tells about another daughter, Akueke, Obierika's child. Her suitor and the celebration of the part of the betrothal ceremony in which the dowry is paid, the uri, are Achebe's subject.

OKONKWO'S ACTIONS

Chielo has returned Ezinma to her parents' compound and Okonkwo's actions of the night before are described - four times he went to Agbala's cave to await Chielo. Apparently Okonkwo had determined that that was where she and Ezinma would eventually turn up and, while he was anxious to be there, he saw no reason to follow the priestess and the child as his wife had (and it would be unbecoming of him to do so). In this story the two contrasting elements in Okonkwo's character are depicted: he had waited until a "reasonable and manly [emphasis mine] interval" had passed - but he had been "gravely worried" about his daughter.

LOOSE COW INCIDENT

The ambiguous relationship between clans members and their traditions that is represented in Okonkwo's actions and emotions during the unsettling night is contrasted by the tale of the cow that got loose and caused some minor damage. In capturing the cow and meting out punishment to her owner for her escape and the damage done, the villagers work together, and they agree to the punishment - a fine in this case - of those whose actions put others in jeopardy.

OKONKWO'S REPUTATION

In a further contrast to his actions of the previous night and to the cow's owner, Okonkwo is singled out by visitors from another village as a prosperous personage and a great warrior, the greatest wrestler and warrior alive, in fact.

THINGS FALL APART

CHAPTER THIRTEEN

. . . .

EZEUDU'S DEATH AND CLAN PHILOSOPHY

The death of Ezeudu provides the narrator with an opportunity to describe a common event in the life of the clan: a funeral.

The funeral also permits the narrator to express the philosophy that underlies all of the clan's activities and beliefs: from birth to death, he says, a man's life is a "series of transition rites which brought him nearer and nearer to his ancestors." An understanding of this philosophy helps the reader realize what motivates Okonkwo and comprehend why traditions and rituals are so important to him. To act correctly, as in the case of Ikemefuna's death, ultimately is more important in this view of human existence than whether Ikemefuna deserves to die or even whether he lives or dies. This attitude is clearly brought into play in the sequence of events that follows.

PRECIPITATING EVENT

During the funeral ritual, the warriors fire their guns into the air. Okonkwo's rifle explodes and a piece of iron pierces the heart of Ezeudu's sixteen-year-old son.

THE PUNISHMENT

Even though everyone realizes that what has transpired was an accident and not Okonkwo's fault, the laws of the clan dictate that he must be exiled for seven years. He must flee from the village because the "crime" that has been committed violates the earth goddess's prohibition of the killing of a clansman. Luckily, the law differentiates between male and female killings. Okonkwo's crime is in the female category because it was inadvertent, so he can return to Umuofia after the requisite amount of time has passed, although his compound must be razed and his livestock killed.

THE CONSEQUENCES

Okonkwo returns to his mother's homeland, the little village of Mbanta, just beyond the borders of Mbaino. Meanwhile, Obierika considers why all this has happened. It is interesting that throughout the novel there are individuals who question (why should a man suffer so grievously for an inadvertent offense?), but it is not until they are exposed to the teachings of Christianity that some of the questioners do anything other than question.

THINGS FALL APART

CHAPTER FOURTEEN

. . . .

OKONKWO'S RECEPTION IN MBANTA

Part Two of *Things Fall Apart* is devoted to an account of Okonkwo's seven-year exile in his motherland. Okonkwo is welcomed to Mbanta by his uncle, Uchendu, and his family, who help him set up his family compound and to settle in.

OKONKWO AND HIS CHI

Okonkwo's great, passionate ambition in life has been to become one of the lords of the clan. With his exile this is no longer possible, and as a result his spirit is partly broken; work is no longer a pleasure for him. Part of his despair must come from the realization that "Clearly his ... chi was not made for great things." "A man cannot rise beyond the destiny of his chi," he reckoned, and the elders saying that if a man said "yea," his chi would affirm him, was not true, for, after all, here he was, "a man whose chi said nay despite his own affirmation." In view of this revelation, Okonkwo's character is summed up by the fact that he still willingly follows the traditional dictates of the clan.

NJIDE'S WEDDING

As there was a funeral portrayed in the previous chapter as part of the picture of village life, in Chapter Fourteen there is a depiction of a marriage ceremony. Although those involved probably never notice, to an outsider it is interesting that virtually all of the social ceremonies that Achebe describes include some sacrificial element. This, too, reflects on Okonkwo's character, for sharing is a built-in component of his culture, as is the implication that no man can ever be entirely free of obligations or can amass an overwhelming fortune. Yams, which area basic ingredient used in determining the worth of an individual in his society, are perishable, and when someone does particularly well, there are celebrations in which they are expected to provide for others according to their wealth. This practice will be seen when Okonkwo prepares to return to Umuofia at the end of his exile, and it is one that he wholeheartedly embraces as a demonstration of his success and the nature of his character.

UCHENDU'S LESSON

When Okonkwo seems to be giving in to his despair, Uchendu counsels him. One's fatherland is best, he says, when things are "sweet," but a man turns to his mother or motherland in times of sorrow and bitterness - and he offends the dead if he refuses to be comforted. It is Okonkwo's duty to comfort his family so that they can return to their home after seven years. Ironically, Uchendu concludes his teaching by stating that he, too, has suffered in his life, as evidenced by his having outlived five wives and twenty-two children but he has never given in and hanged himself. Okonkwo's fate will be different.

PHILOSOPHY IN SONG

The chapter concludes with Uchendu's quoting of two lines from the song that is sung when a woman dies: "For whom is it well, for whom is it well?/There is no one for whom it is well." The pessimism of the philosophy expressed in this song parallels the fundamental philosophy outlined in the previous chapter.

THINGS FALL APART

CHAPTER FIFTEEN

OBIERIKA'S VISIT

In the second year of Okonkwo's exile, his friend Obierika visits him and tells a tale about the destruction of the village of Abame. The first white man appeared, "riding an iron horse" (a bicycle). The Oracle said that he would break up their clan and bring destruction, so they killed the white man; the Oracle also claimed that there were other white men on the way. The Oracle was correct in both instances, though not in the way in which his warning was interpreted. The white man spoke to the villagers, but because of the Oracle's warning that the white man would bring destruction, he was killed. The villagers did not understand the white man's words, just as they will not understand his culture, nor did the white man understand them. This lack of communication and understanding is vital, since in the final analysis it forces the sides into an adversarial confrontation rather than allowing them to coexist.

The **irony** of the situation is that the villagers kill the white man thinking that they can thereby avoid the destruction that the Oracle has foretold, but when three of his companions visit the village and see his bicycle tied to a sacred silk-cotton tree, they know what has taken place and they return later, on a market day, and massacre almost every member of the tribe. Thus it is that the Oracle's warning comes true.

There is an additional **irony** involved in this sequence of events. Earlier in the novel the market at Abame had been the source of envy for some of the characters who were displeased at the village's success.

ABSENTEE FARMING

Following the comment that others may be worse off than Okonkwo, there is evidence of how true this is, especially given the events of Abame, when Obierika gives his friend the money that he has earned from the yams that Okonkwo left behind in Umuofia. In spite of his suffering, Okonkwo is still prospering, thanks to the help of his loyal friend. The riches that he gains in this manner allow him to leave Mbanta in high esteem and return to Umuofia with his head held high.

THINGS FALL APART

CHAPTER SIXTEEN

....

OBIERIKA RETURNS

In the fourth year of Okonkwo's exile, Obierika again visits him. Meanwhile, Christian missionaries have arrived in Umuofia. The African view of the converts, those who have accepted the white man's god, is that none was a "man of title" - they were efulefu ("worthless, empty men") not respected by the clan before the coming of the white man.

NWOYE'S CONVERSION

Sadly for Okonkwo, he learns that Nwoye has become a missionary convert. The story of Nwoye and Okonkwo's estrangement follows.

MISSIONARIES IN MBANTA

Six missionaries arrive in Mbanta, one of whom is a white man. An Ibo man who serves as the white man's interpreter explains about Christianity; the clansmen are derisive, but the singing of an evangelical song stops them. The power that the song has over them undoubtedly grows out of the Ibo culture's love of song. Okonkwo argues against the single-god concept saying that it cannot be valid if there was a son. The concept of the Trinity is seen as evidence of the madness of the white missionary. However, Nwoye is captivated by the poetry of the new religion (embodied in the hymn that was sung). This, combined with his questions about the murder of twin children and innocents such as Ikemefuna which had been linked in his mind at the time of his friend's death, is sufficient to persuade him to adopt the new ways. Those things that cause Okonkwo to cling to his lifestyle are the same things that drive Nwoye away from it.

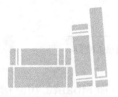

THINGS FALL APART

. . . .

"EVILFOREST" PLOT

The missionaries request that the village give them a plot of land upon which they can build their church. Uchendu suggests that they give a part of the village's "evil forest," the place where those who died of leprosy, smallpox, and other dreaded causes are buried. This will surely do them in, he reasons. But, Uchendu's plan backfires, for when the missionaries do not die within four days, the villagers believe that the white man's power must be great and they begin to convert. Amusingly, they believe that his eyeglasses enable him to talk to spirits.

NWOYE'S CONVERSION DETAILED

When Okonkwo learns that Nwoye has been seen among the Christians, he beats his son, who leaves. Indeed, adding salt to the wound, Nwoye plans to return and convert his mother and brothers and sisters to Christianity. Okonkwo, who has fought to preserve the traditions of his clan and family, succeeds in alienating those whom he is trying to protect.

OKONKWO'S CHI

Okonkwo sees all of the misfortune that is befalling him as being instigated by his chi. The true horror for him is that when he dies, there will be no one to worship and sacrifice at the ancestral shrine. Not only will the ancestors be let down, but so will he, and all of his life will have been a hollow mockery.

THINGS FALL APART

CHAPTER EIGHTEEN

....

THE WHITE MAN'S GOVERNMENT

The church continues to prosper, and there is a rumor about the existence of the white man's government. In a kind of preparatory note, as evidence of the power of the white man's government, a story is told about a man who had killed a missionary and been hanged for his crime. This is a **foreshadowing** of what will happen to Okonkwo.

THE OSU CONFLICT

There is a conflict in the local church over the status of osu, the outcasts. Mr. Kiaga's strength holds the congregation together and the osu are admitted as members of the congregation.

HOLY PYTHON

Later, one of the osu converts kills the village's sacred python. Okonkwo advises the villagers to drive the church membership out of the village. Instead, it is decided to ostracize the Christians. The murder of the clan's holy python is highly symbolic, both in the action itself and in the lack of serious reaction that it brings from the gods. That such a transgression can go unpunished has a disquieting effect on the villagers, who mount their own campaign against the Christians.

EASTER WEEK CONFRONTATION

In an unprecedented move, women converts are denied access to the water supply of the village's stream. Okoli, the osu convert accused of killing the royal python (an act that he denies), dies - and the clan sees this as evidence that their gods are still powerful; they stop harassing the Christians.

THINGS FALL APART

CHAPTER NINETEEN

· ·

END OF THE EXILE

The name of Okonkwo's first son born to him while he is in exile indicates the warrior's state of mind, for the child is called "Begotten in the Wilderness," although Mbanta clearly is not a wilderness, even in comparison with Umuofia.

The end of the seven years has come, however, and Okonkwo makes preparations to return to Umuofia. In spite of his strong wish to return, though, he does not do so early because that would diminish his justly imposed punishment. Okonkwo is a man of honor, and he willingly accepts whatever is imposed upon him by his society, abiding by the rules to the minutest point.

FAREWELL FEAST

Before leaving Mbanta to return to Umuofia, Okonkwo hosts a magnificent feast to show his gratitude to his mother's family and those who helped him in his time of need (and he refuses to be niggardly in the foods that he provides, despite his wives' urging).

The importance of the concept of kinship is expressed and illustrated by this farewell feast. All of the descendants of Ikolo, all of the Umunna, are invited. By virtue of Okonkwo's performance in hosting this feast that exceeds all expectations, his clansmen recognize that he is the speaker for the clan's traditional values.

THINGS FALL APART

. . . .

OKONKWO'S RESILIENCE

Okonkwo's resilient spirit is evidenced by the fact that even during the first year of his exile he was making plans for the return to his home village. This spirit helps him overcome the tragedy of his first son's conversion to Christianity. Perhaps the loss of his son is partly offset by the maturing of his favorite daughter, Ezinma, who over the seven years has grown to be such a beautiful woman that she is called "Crystal of Beauty," as her mother had been years before.

RETURN FROM EXILE

When Okonkwo returns to Umuofia, however, he finds that some of his plans will be thwarted by circumstances beyond his control. Chief among these is the change wrought by the coming of the white men: the establishment of the church

(Oguefi Ugonna became the first titled villager to convert) and the intrusion of a new governmental structure and concept of justice evidenced by the establishment of a court and the appointment of a District Commissioner.

RATIONALE

Okonkwo asks why the villagers do not throw the white men out. Obierika replies that it is already too late for that course of action - their "own men and ... sons" have already joined the ranks of the strangers. In addition, if the villagers drive out the two who are there, others would come, with soldiers, and Umuofia would become another Abame, the neighboring village that was destroyed in revenge for the murder of a white man.

THE KEY PHRASE

Oftentimes an author will include a key line or phrase in a literary work that epitomizes the main **theme** of the work. This occurs in *Things Fall Apart* when it is further explained that the white men do not understand the clan's customs about the land, that they do not even speak their language. This observation leads Obierika to the conclusion that sums up the events in the novel: the white man "has put a knife on the things that held us together and we have fallen apart." While this explicit statement might have been omitted by Achebe as a more mature author, nevertheless it clearly explains what has happened to the fabric of clan traditions, and it does so in a phrasing that is appropriately African.

A HANGING

The story of the hanging of Aneto for killing Oduche in a land dispute is related. The land was given to Nname's family, presumably because he had supported the white man. This tale serves to define the white man's punishment for murder so, when he commits murder later, Okonkwo is already aware of what the consequences will be. This may partly explain why he hangs himself - even in death he will not allow the white man to control him.

THINGS FALL APART

CHAPTER TWENTY-ONE

· ·

MONEY

As a social comment, the narrator notes that the coming of the white men and their "new dispensation," an obvious reference to Yeats' poem, was not unappealing to all of Umuofia's inhabitants, for the value of local products increased and money flowed into the village as the economy prospered.

Throughout the novel Achebe presents both the good and the bad prospects of the events that transpire. Although there is a tendency to romanticize the old and denigrate the new, the author demonstrates that not all of the old was admirable (the killing of twin babies) just as not all of the new is reprehensible (a more humane acceptance of all people as equals).

ENOCH

Enoch, we should recall, was the son of the snake cult priest and there was a rumor that he had killed the sacred python and eaten it.

MR. BROWN

The white missionary, Mr. Brown, gains respect in the village through his tolerance of others and refusal to sanction acts such as Enoch's. Akunna, a great man from a neighboring village, gives his one son to Mr. Brown so that the youth can learn the white man's knowledge at the school that Brown has established.

RELIGIOUS DEBATE

A religious debate is described, in which Brown and Akunna discuss the nature of Christianity and the pagan religion of the god Chukwu. In this way, not only does Brown learn about the religion of the region so that he can combat it in a nonviolent way, but Achebe provides an explanation of those beliefs for his readers.

Brown's actions are contrary to what Obierika had claimed, that the white man did not know or care about the Ibo ways, and they are useful because he employs the knowledge that he gains in these conversations to persuade the villagers, who came to learn, to join his church.

BROWN'S HEALTH

Indeed, in his efforts to proceed peacefully, Brown overtaxes himself to the point where his health begins to fail. This is an important plot development, given the nature of the man who will replace him and how his replacement will have an effect on Okonkwo's life.

OKONKWO'S RETURN

Part of the effect on Okonkwo is prepared for by the juxtaposition of Brown's successful efforts and the revelation that Nwoye has taken the name Isaac. Nothing is more personal than an individual's name, so in adopting a new name, Nwoye/Isaac has demonstrated the depth of his conversion and rejection of his father's beliefs and ways.

The choice of the name Isaac is replete with Biblically symbolic values that pertain to Achebe's novel. Isaac is the son of Abraham, whose outstanding characteristic is his faith in God and with whom God made the sacred covenant (Genesis 22 and following). Thus, Abraham is considered by Jews as the Father of the Faithful and the founder of their people. As the ultimate test of Abraham's faith, God ordered him to sacrifice the son of his old age, Isaac. At the last moment, just as the father had placed his bound son upon an altar and taken up his knife to slay him, the angel of the Lord intervened, saying that Abraham had proven his faith: a ram was sacrificed in Isaac's place. Okonkwo is characterized throughout the novel in terms that would apply to Abraham. It might even be said that Okonkwo was literally willing to sacrifice the lives of Ikemefuna and Ezinma and to disown Nwoye because of his faith in the tribe's traditions and laws.

Abraham, like Okonkwo, suffers mightily during his lifetime, forced by drought and other disasters to travel throughout many lands. It is Abraham who seeks deliverance from the destruction of Sodom for his nephew, Lot, and his nephew's family. Disturbed because Sarah, his wife, has borne him no sons (one of Okonkwo's underlying concerns is with Nwoye's image as a "man"), Abraham lies with Sarah's handmaiden, Hagar, who gives birth to Ishmael. Hager and Ishmael are banished from Abraham's household and Ishmael becomes the father of the Ishmaelites.

Subsequently, Abraham fathers Isaac with Sarah. In turn, Isaac and Rebekah become the parents of the twins Esau and Jacob (Genesis 25). Rebekah is the daughter of Bethuel, the Aramean of Paddan-aram, a woman from another tribe. When she is with child the Lord proclaims to her, "Two nations are in your womb, and two peoples, born of you, shall be divided; the one shall be stronger than the other." And, so it is with Okonkwo's divided people; one group will come to dominate the other.

NWOYE AS ISAAC

Some Biblical scholars feel that the two brothers represent a cluster of religiously based tribal traditions. Esau, the hunter and beloved of his father, is robbed of his birthright (in exchange for some lentil pottage) by Jacob, a quiet man and his mother's favorite. The brothers become estranged, though they are later reconciled. Esau becomes the father of the Edomite nation; Jacob is Joseph's father. As related to *Things Fall Apart*, Nwoye as Isaac might be seen as carrying within himself the divided nation of Nigeria, the split between the old hunting society and the quieter Christian culture; he is the descendent of a primal patriarchal system.

There is further reinforcing evidence of how things are falling apart and how Okonkwo is out of joint with the time when his return is not as triumphant as he had planned. Instead, his return largely goes unrecognized. Some of the things that he had planned cannot take place purely because the timing is wrong (as in his inability to have his sons initiated into the ozo society, it being the wrong year for the ritual to take place).

The final paragraph of the chapter shows that Okonkwo's grief is not just personal but also for his clan; he mourns that the warriors of Umuofia have become soft and womanlike, the ultimate degeneration in his perception of the world. At this point all of the elements have come together that will inexorably lead to the demise of Okonkwo and his way of life.

THINGS FALL APART

CHAPTER TWENTY-TWO

· ·

THE REVEREND SMITH'S INFLUENCE

Mr. Brown's successor is the Reverend James Smith, a man very unlike his predecessor. The opposite of Brown, Smith sees everything in terms of duality: something is "either/or," "black or white" - and black is evil. He sees the world as a battlefield and believes in "slaying the prophets of Baal." Over-zealous converts such as Enoch can now flourish.

UNMASKING

Smith's presence leads to an event that is unparalleled in the history of the tribe. During the annual ceremony held in honor of the earth deity, Enoch publicly unmasks an egwugwu. Such an action is a symbolic killing of the ancestral spirit, and a confrontation between the pagan and Christian religions is unavoidable (and perhaps sought by Smith). The hiding of

Enoch in the parsonage further emphasizes the symbolic nature of his action, as does the revenge of the egwugwu, who come to participate in the destruction of Enoch's compound. Achebe's ability as a storyteller is exemplified in this section as the excitement of the situation is translated into action.

DESTRUCTION OF THE CHURCH

Ajofia, the leading egwugwu of Umuofia, tells Smith that, because they liked his predecessor, they would spare his life, but that they must destroy the church. The clan's understanding of the symbolism of the unmasking is thus demonstrated. An understanding of the importance of religion in a man's life is demonstrated as well when Ajofia shows the tolerance that Smith is not capable of, saying that Smith is still welcome to stay in the village and to worship his own god, for it is good for a man to worship the god of his fathers. The church is then destroyed.

THINGS FALL APART

CHAPTER TWENTY-THREE

OKONKWO'S SATISFACTION

For the first time in years, Okonkwo begins to feel better about the coming of the white man because the clan seems to be regaining its correct, traditional course. Furthermore, although they did not agree with his counsel, they had listened with respect to his opinions and advice. The **irony** is that just when things seem to be brightening for him, they are about to become darkest.

BETRAYAL

The District Commissioner calls the village's six leaders, Okonkwo among them, to meet with him to discuss the recent events. He then uses trickery to bring in twelve of his own men who capture the six visitors. Since the meeting was conducted under the guise of diplomacy, a host has an obligation to protect his guests, and the introduction of the Commissioner's men was brought about through duplicity; the white man's actions are abhorrent.

INSULT UPON INSULT

To add insult to injury, literally, the commissioner levies a fine of two hundred bags of cowries to be delivered to him by the village in order to buy the release of his prisoners. The most degrading insult comes when the prison barber shaves their heads. Then the court messengers joke about the captives' titles - earlier Okonkwo had spoken derisively about a neighboring village where titles were taken lightly, and the messengers unjustly apply this same obloquy to the Umuofian leaders.

COURT MESSENGERS

Despite the District Commissioner's assurance to the contrary, the captives are physically punished by the court messengers. For three days they are taunted, denied water, and beaten. As might be anticipated, the messengers demand two hundred and fifty bags of cowries from the villagers for the prisoners' release. This treatment is so unconscionable that Umuofia reacts like a startled animal, its "ears erect, sniffing the silent, ominous air and not knowing which way to run." Clearly a motive has been established for whatever action Okonkwo might take later.

THINGS FALL APART

CHAPTER TWENTY-FOUR

TOWN MEETING

When the cowries are paid, the prisoners are freed. A town meeting is held to debate the course of action to be followed. The debate is so crucial that virtually every one of the villagers is in attendance; the narrator claims that there are so many people present that a grain of sand thrown into the air could not fall to the ground, an indication that the Umuofians comprehend the significance of what has transpired.

DEBATE

Okonkwo feels so strongly that war must be declared that he determines to go his own way if this is not the path the clan chooses. Okika, one of the freed prisoners, speaks, telling his listeners that the clan's life is at stake. But the concept of having to fight with their own clansmen, those who have converted to

Christianity, is introduced. Although not developed, this idea contains within it the implied destruction of the clan; if there is a civil war, the clan can never be the same again, since clansmen do not fight one another. Yet, if there is no fight, then the clan has already lost its identity to those who have renounced it. For Okonkwo, there will be no choice; he must defend fiercely and physically that which he believes in, as has been prepared for throughout the narrative and as will be manifest in the next sequence of actions.

THE BEHEADING

As Okika is speaking, the court messengers come with orders from the white man "whose power you know too well" to stop the meeting. In a flash, Okonkwo beheads the head messenger with his machete. From the very beginning of the novel Okonkwo's character has been developed so that such an action is predictable, and probably unavoidable, under these circumstances. He does not have, nor does he take, the time to think things through. He merely acts in anger to the insult and to the threat to his beliefs. When the villagers do not react as one and kill the remaining messengers, he realizes that the tumult and commotion represent the confused spirit of his clan, that it can no longer protect itself from outsiders. At this moment, he also realizes that he is alone and that his fate is sealed. There can be no turning back; it has been established how the white men react to the murder of one of their own, whether an African or a European.

THINGS FALL APART

CHAPTER TWENTY-FIVE

OKONKWO'S SUICIDE

The final chapter opens with the arrival of the District Commissioner and a band of soldiers at Umuofia. They are met by Obierika, who requests that they help him. Obierika leads the group into the bush where he asks the strangers to take Okonkwo's body down from the tree where he has hanged himself and bury it, for the taking of one's own life is an abomination. This may be the ultimate tragedy for Okonkwo, the man who more than anyone else in the novel is concerned with preserving the customs of his ancestors and his gods. As would be the case in Catholicism or other Christian religions, suicide is the one unforgiven sin - the self-murderer has taken the god's prerogative but, moreover, he cannot repent and beg forgiveness. Thus, Okonkwo has consciously cut himself off in life and in death from that which he was fighting to preserve. It is a terrible irony.

THE DISTRICT COMMISSIONER'S BOOK

The District Commissioner, who has no real idea who Okonkwo is, becomes interested in this case as something more than a bureaucratic problem when he learns the significance of the old warrior's act. Unfortunately, his interest is minimal; the District Commissioner thinks that the story might be included as a paragraph in a book that he is writing about his experiences in Africa.

The reduction of Okonkwo's life to a paragraph is not the final irony, however. The last sentence in *Things Fall Apart* reveals the title of the Commissioner's book. It is to be called *The Pacification of the Primitive Tribes of the Lower Niger.*

THE CONCLUSION

The novel's concluding paragraph is filled with meaning that has been gathering from the first sentence of the book. The District Commissioner sees Okonkwo's death in terms of what has happened to the man, not in relation to the entire clan, because the idea of clan does not exist in the white man's world. The different emphases in the African and European religions demonstrate this; the clan is related, held together by gods, common ancestors, and traditions, all bearing on every facet of the clan members' lives. In Christianity, as evidenced in the religion of the English invaders, the same general things are operative, but the religion is much more abstract, not so personal or so intimately involved on a daily basis with everything that an individual does and thinks. Certainly the Christianity of Mssrs. Brown, Kiaga, and Smith involves a god intimately involved with them on an individual basis, yet Europe is too large for the beliefs to have the same immediacy that they have among

Okonkwo's clansmen. Therefore, the Commissioner and the Reverend Mr. Smith do not grieve for what is lost or for the dead Okonkwo. The concept that "no man is an island" does not seem to apply for them.

THE SIGNIFICANCE OF THE FINAL PARAGRAPH

By referring to the subject and title of the District Commissioner's book, Achebe demonstrates that it is not just a man's honor and life that have been destroyed by the impact of an invading culture. In effect, Okonkwo symbolizes his whole tribe, which has had the same thing happen to them, i.e., they have become emasculated, they are no longer a tribe. To the Commissioner, all of this is only interesting as an anecdote. The story is not considered important enough to warrant a full chapter (though Achebe finds enough in it to write an entire novel). That the District Commissioner does not understand the human element in what he has witnessed and is participating in is exemplified in the case-study title of his book.

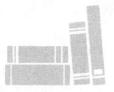

THINGS FALL APART

. . . .

In many respects, *Things Fall Apart* is simply the tale of an individual's inability to reconcile himself with the introduction of a new culture into an established social setting. He sees no possibility of his traditional culture incorporating elements from and merging with the intruding culture to create a new society. Instead, the only possibility that he sees is the destruction of one of the societies. As a result, the novel focuses upon the protagonist, Ogbuefi Okonkwo. The fact that Achebe's interests centers on Okonkwo can be seen not merely from his exclusion of full-drawn portraits of the other figures who are presented in the story but also from the way in which those characters are used: Okonkwo is the principal, and all of the others are shown primarily only insofar as they interact with Okonkwo or as they shed light on his character. (This includes, of course, mentions of people whose histories in one way or another contribute to an understanding of the nature of the society that Okonkwo is trying to defend.)

Neither Ikemefuna nor Unoka, for example, is fully developed in his own right, and they assume little individuality or importance in the book except on a superficial level.

Although they are talked about by the narrator, not much space is devoted to them as acting people. Even Nwoye never acquires the proportions of much more than a two-dimensional figure. Essentially, each character is of interest only when he or she comes in contact with Okonkwo, and then that interest occurs almost entirely because they are coming in contact with him. The rest of the time these other characters are ignored. Once the action containing them has passed, they are discarded (as in the instance of Maduka, and the majority of the characters who appear in the novel), and even when they are present, the characterizing touches that Achebe provides are usually those that have some obvious connection with Okonkwo - we learn little or nothing else about the nature of those who inhabit Okonkwo's universe except that which reflects Okonkwo himself or his culture. In part, of course, this is due to the fact that *Things Fall Apart* is Okonkwo's story.

OKONKWO AS SYMBOL

By centering on Okonkwo, the writer has essentially symbolized an entire society, and it was the latter that was his purpose; in Okonkwo's fall we can see the effect of the imposition of a new culture on an already established society. If Achebe had tried to depict a hoard of full-blown characters representing every facet of the social order, the novel would have become a Dickensian work full of characters rather than a novel centering on ideas, a novel about individual people instead of an examination of how certain universal kinds of events impact upon everyone. Because he chose to write about a common experience, what he says about nineteenth-century Africa is applicable to twentieth-century Western culture, or any culture at any time.

OGBUEFI OKONKWO

Because *Things Fall Apart* is a novel about a symbolic character who represents an entire culture, there is no physical description presented of Okonkwo, other than the general information that he is large and strong. In addition, he never comments on his emotions, he only says what he thinks, though the narrator often tells us what Okonkwo's feeling are.

The "Roaring Flame," as Okonkwo was known, grew up in impoverished conditions brought about by his father's laziness and inability to plan ahead. As a result, Okonkwo came to hate and fear those qualities that he saw resident in his father. He was highly motivated to succeed, as a young wrestler, as a warrior, as a farmer, as a clan leader, and as a husband and father. Because of this powerful drive, he overcame his beginnings and rose to the top in most of these categories. As a "man of action, a man of war" who could "stand the look of blood," Okonkwo "brought honor to his village" (p. 14).

Still, his life was dominated by his "fear of failure and of weakness" (p. 16). It is this fact that really sets Okonkwo off from those around him. His every action is dictated by these twin fears, which is why he participates in Ikemefuna's murder. Of course, it can be argued that his actions are governed by his reverence for the clan's traditions, and indeed he does come to symbolize his culture, but these two elements are related; if he were not so fearful, if he were not so intransigent in his adherence to his cultural heritage, it may be that he could have found a way to adjust to the impinging of a new culture on the old. The adamancy with which Okonkwo holds to his clan's traditional values is admirable, yet there is a suggestion that part of his motivation stems from his fear of failure - the absolutes of his heritage protect him from everything; the traditions give answers to all situations that might arise, and he can lead his life comfortably in unquestioning obedience.

In the end, Okonkwo not only represents his culture but in his tragic destruction as an individual he also reflects the elements within his culture that will lead to its disintegration, those inhumane and unbending components that were necessary for survival at one time in the clan's history but which are no longer viable. The flame is an heroic and spectacular aspect of the Ibo mentality, but the water of Christianity overflows it easily and virtually unknowingly. Those who can adapt to the new circumstances as they evolve go on to create a new culture, part Ibo and part Christian. Those who cannot adapt are destroyed. Okonkwo is one of the latter. We can admire him as a person and his background as they combine to form a symbol for something that was once relatively bright and shining, but the elements that made Okonkwo and his society so lustrous are the same elements that carry the seeds of self-destruction. A lesser man might have bent, yielded, and survived. Nonetheless, in the final analysis, Okonkwo and his culture have been replaced.

UNOKA

Okonkwo's father, Unoka is a lazy, improvident, fun-loving, carefree man who is incapable of providing for himself or his family. Although he has an irresistible spirit and is artistic, these are not qualities that are admired in his clan because they do not help either the man or the clan survive in its present stage of development. He becomes a debtor and palm-wine drunkard. Unoka's failures and limitations are important in the development of his son's character, however, for they provide a standard against which Okonkwo measures himself and from which the younger man is constantly fleeing. It is in contrast to Unoka that Okonkwo's character is defined.

NWOYE

Twelve years old when the novel begins, Nwoye is Okonkwo's eldest son. The hope of his father turns to despair, however, for Nwoye soon evidences a "soft" nature reminiscent of his grandfather, Unoka.

Admittedly, Okonkwo's reactions to his son are based on his desire that the boy become self-sufficient and successful. Nevertheless, because his father treats him harshly when he is seen to be less of a "man" than Okonkwo desires his son to be and because Nwoye has the ability to see injustices in the world about him, he questions tribal customs. This makes him vulnerable to the message that the missionaries preach and he converts to Christianity. Not only does he reject his father's society in his conversion, but he rejects his entire heritage when he adopts the name Isaac.

IKEMEFUNA

A young boy from Mbaino, Ikemefuna is brought to Umuofia as part of the recompense made by the neighboring village for the murder of Udo's wife. A lively, popular, knowledgeable lad, he soon becomes attached to Nwoye and is treated by Okonkwo's family as though he is part of the family, even to the point of his calling Okonkwo "father."

After Ikemefuna has resided in Okonkwo's household for three years, Chielo, the priestess of Agbala, declares that the hostage must be put to death. Okonkwo participates in the killing, delivering the death blow himself. Ikemefuna's death is a major factor in turning Nwoye away from his heritage.

EKWEFI

Okonkwo's second wife, Ekwefi is about forty-five years old. Previously married, she was so impressed by Okonkwo's prowess as a wrestler that she left her first husband and moved in with him. She is the most clearly drawn female character presented in the novel, and in some ways appears to be the complement of her husband.

Ekwefi is particularly important in providing a contrast to Okonkwo in her eagerness to express her emotions, especially when related to her daughter, Ezinma. This trait humanizes Ekwefi's character for the reader more than perhaps any other character in the novel, establishing a broader base for evaluating the Ibo people and their culture than might be garnered from exposure to Okonkwo alone. It is vital to Achebe's purpose that this occur or else the generalizing effect might be lost, limiting the application of the **themes** expressed in his work.

EZINMA

The only child of Ekwefi and Okonkwo, Ezinma is her father's favorite daughter. When she is introduced at the beginning of the novel, she is an inquisitive, eager young girl of ten. At the conclusion of the story she is a beautiful young lady. In spite of occasional physical illnesses, her spirit carries her through, and she has many of the attributes that Okonkwo wishes that Nwoye possessed. It is the relationship between Ezinma and

her mother that is so important in developing the huma.
characteristics of the Ibos in *Things Fall Apart*, and he.
relationship with her father gives us a glimpse of the man as he
might have been if he had not been so badly traumatized by his
own father's perceived failures.

OBIERIKA

Okonkwo's best friend, Obierika supplies another contrast to
the **protagonist**. Since his background in the culture is similar
to Okonkwo's and since he is equally successful, it is interesting
to see how his reactions to events portrayed in the novel, and
specifically to the coming of the white man, differ from those of
his friend.

It is revealing that Obierika does not follow Okonkwo's
path. On the one hand, it is apparent that some with similar
backgrounds will survive. This indicates that at least part of
what is involved in Okonkwo's fall derives from his personal
background (i.e., his father's influence on his life) as opposed to
being endemic to the culture from which he comes. On the other
hand, Obierika does not achieve the heroic status that Okonkwo
does when he chooses death at his own hands rather than life in
a world that has lost its way.

THE VILLAGE AS A CHARACTER

Although not a person, the village of Umuofia in many ways
functions as a major character in Achebe's novel. Umuofia is the
culture that defines Okonkwo and his fellow Ibos, and the author
carefully details life within the village throughout *Things Fall
Apart*. It is a presence that impacts on all involved in the tale.

THINGS FALL APART

. . . .

SIGNIFICANCE OF THE NOVEL'S TITLE

First published in 1920, William Butler Yeats' poem, "The Second Coming," is the source of the title for Achebe's novel. The title is, therefore, a literary allusion.

A Literary Allusion is a reference to another literary work or character. This device serves as a sort of literary shorthand because the reference somehow expands the meaning of the work in which the allusion is incorporated; it allows the reader to understand in more depth what is being discussed. In the case of this novel, for instance, readers familiar with Yeats' poem would understand the emotional and intellectual significance of what transpires before they ever read the novel, and Achebe can thus refrain from spelling out in great detail what Yeats has already said. A literary allusion, then, serves to impart Connotations (meanings that go beyond the simple face value of the words) based on shared literary experiences.

YEATS' THEORY OF CYCLES

Yeats' poem illustrates the poet's theory about the circularity of time and history. According to *The Norton Anthology of English Literature* (5th ed., "The Major Authors," M. H. Abrams, Gen. Ed., New York: W. W. Norton, 1987, p. 2308), "The Second Coming" expresses the poet's "sense of the dissolution of the civilization of his time, the end of one cycle of history, and the approach of another. He called each cycle of history a 'gyre' (line 1) - literally a circular or spiral turn. The birth of Christ brought to an end the cycle that had lasted from what Yeats called the "Babylonian mathematical starlight' (2000 B.C.) to the dissolution of Greco-Roman culture." In his prose work, *A Vision*, Yeats had posed the question that underlies his poem: "What if the circle begin again?" Furthermore, he wondered. "What if the irrational return?" and he suggested that "we may be about to accept the most implacable authority the world has known." Naturally, Yeats was concerned about events taking place during the first quarter of the twentieth century, those things that would directly impact upon his own culture, yet it is evident from the poem that the basic concept that he expresses would apply to any society at any time.

As a result of Achebe's use of Yeats' phrase, the African using the Irishman's words, the meaning of the novel is expanded and generalized. As demonstrated above, Achebe's **themes** definitely relate to the intrusion of the white man on African culture, but if that were all that were involved, the novel might be read only by those interested in the anthropological and sociological elements that it incorporates. Instead, *Things Fall Apart* is considered a major work of world literature, and the title exemplifies in part why this is so-although the event is specifically African, the experience is universally human. Achebe used a phrase from T. S. Eliot's poem, "The Magi," as a title for his second novel, *No Longer at Ease*, for a similar effect, appropriate since the second novel deals with the confusion experienced by Okonkwo's grandson, Obi, as he tries to come to grips with the civilization that replaced that of his forefathers.

CONTEXT OF THINGS FALL APART

The opening **stanza** of "The Second Coming" depicts civilization as it is just before the new forces appear. It is a terrifying picture:

> **Turning and turning in the widening gyre**
> **The falcon cannot hear the falconer;**
> **Things fall apart; the center cannot hold;**
> **Mere anarchy is loosed upon the world,**
> **The blood-dimmed tide is loosed, and everywhere**
> **The ceremony of innocence is drowned;**
> **The best lack all conviction, while the worst**
> **Are full of passionate intensity.**

Yeats' title refers to what most of his audience would assume would be a liberating and joyous event, the Second Coming of Christ at the end of the world when all true believers would be taken to Heaven. Instead of the anticipated joy, however, Yeats presents a picture of what would happen if the Second Coming were the return of the forces of paganism that preceded Christ's first appearance on Earth. The event would be so awful that the poet can only describe it by saying that in contrast what is happening now is "Mere anarchy." Since anarchy is defined as "Absence of any cohering principle" and political disorder and confusion" (*The American Heritage Dictionary*, 2nd ed., Boston: Houghton Mifflin, 1976), the modifier "mere" indicates how horrible what is to follow must be.

By the same token, many would assume that the introduction of western civilization on the African continent would be something that would be welcomed and bring with it untold benefits. Achebe says that this may not be true and he utilizes the resources of a powerful literary **allusion** to provide added depth to his own words and thoughts. Since there is an ironic tone to "The Second Coming," it is not surprising that Achebe's novel also is filled with **irony**. There is a kind of double irony involved as well, though, in that Yeats writes about the replacement of Christianity by paganism whereas Achebe writes about a pre-Christian culture is ousted and supplanted by Christianity. Those for whom Yeats' poem would be upsetting are thus faced with a particularly poignant dilemma when the second **stanza** of "The Second Coming" is interpreted through the eyes of one whose salvation is denied by the very elements that normally, in the western universe, would be considered a saving grace and the road to salvation.

OTHER PARALLELS

Yeats' description of the awakening of a different civilization certainly contains within it some of the emotions, realizations, and nightmares that Okonkwo underwent:

> **Surely some revelation is at hand;**
> **Surely the Second Coming is at hand.**
> **The Second Coming! Hardly are those words out**
> **When a vast image out of Spiritus Mundi**
> **Troubles my sight: somewhere in sands of the desert**
> **A shape with lion body and the head of a man,**
> **A gaze blank and pitiless as the sun,**
> **Is moving its slow thighs, while all about it**
> **Reel shadows of the indignant desert birds.**

The darkness drops again; but now I know
That twenty centuries of stony sleep
Were vexed to nightmare by a rocking cradle,
And what rough beast, its hour come round at last,
Slouches towards Bethlehem to be born?

The juxtaposition of Yeats and Achebe thus undermines the traditional European view of Africa and presents historical events from a reverse perspective. The revelation provided Christians by Yeats' work is turned back upon them when they apply the poetic musings to Okonkwo and discover how interchangeable the events are. The final parallel in the poem, the image of the beast that slouches towards Bethlehem, the birthplace of Jesus, to be born is intended to make the reader realize the enormity of Yeats' vision, and it serves to reinforce Achebe's vision too. Being concerned with truth and dignity, however, Achebe does not stop here in creating a parallel in *Things Fall Apart*. Even if one were to reverse the religions of Yeats' poem so that the pagan creed is to be replaced by Christianity, the universal meaning is the same, and Achebe recognizes this point in his reversal in the novel. While it is the society that he focuses upon, it is also the concept of displacement that occupies the author.

THINGS FALL APART AND NO LONGER AT EASE: A COMPARISON

A study of anthropological or sociological examinations of traditional Ibo societies, especially as they existed before the coming of the white man, will provide the student with a vivid picture of the kind of culture and the intertribal relationships referred to in the "Introduction" of this study. It is evident, both from the novelist's essays and interviews and from his novels, that Achebe is concerned with the conflict between the old and the new and that he sees the resultant loss of tribal identity and cultural values on the part of the Ibo as being tragic in nature (see Robert Serumaga's "Interview with Chinua Achebe," *Cultural Events in Africa*, No. 28, London, Transcription Centre, 1967).

The areas that are particularly valuable to consider involve: (1) the comparison between Obi and his heroic grandfather; (2) the picture of the uncorrupted village life and tribal ways contrasted with the corruption of modern Lagos; and (3), an extension of (2), the tribal cultural values that have been destroyed, all of which are clearer when the two books are read in conjunction with one another for each novel provides valuable comments on the **themes** of the other. As a matter of fact, it might have been easy to dismiss Achebe's writing as an oversentimentalized, romantic, Rousseau-like view of the "Noble Savage," of the "good olde days," were it not for the inclusion of descriptions of some of the less admirable and more unpleasant traits of village life. His novels gain stature when it can be seen that he has a sense of objectivity, clearly brought out when the two novels are read together. We also are impressed by the universality of his **theme** and the realization that Achebe is not talking just about Ibos confronting change but about the plight of all people who are faced with fundamental changes in their societies.

BIRTH AND DEATH: DUALITY

In *Things Fall Apart* Okonkwo fought heroically to defend a way of life and a religion that was an integral part of that lifestyle. The coming of the white man was the birth of a new period in the history of Nigeria, but Achebe's novel suggests that birth and death are a duality, imposing the anthropologically described pattern whereby the old-year king must be defeated by the new-year king before the latter can insure a good harvest in an agriculturally oriented community, such as the Ibo were before the white man intruded. (See Northup Frye's *The Anatomy of Criticism* and Francis Cornford's *The Origin of Attic Comedy* for interesting discussions of how these patterns have become incorporated into literary patterns and stereotypes.) The introduction of new cultural elements may constitute a birth, then, but it also means the death (i.e., destruction) of certain conflicting or less forceful traditional elements. Achebe is well aware of the kind of paradox that preoccupied John Donne and which is at the base of much Eastern philosophy and religion-life can only come from death and vice versa.

A Paradox is a seemingly self-contradictory statement that is actually true. John Donne's metaphysical poetry abounds with examples of paradox, as in his "Holy Sonnet xviii" when he says to God, "I/ Expect You enthrall me, never shall be free,/ Nor ever chaste, except You ravish me."

Thus, the novel becomes an allegory for all people who are born into a new way of life at the cost of their old ways.

An Allegory is a story in which a literal person, object, abstract idea, or event symbolically stands both for itself and for something else. In a sense, an allegory is a kind of extended metaphor through which the author is trying to express certain concepts or actions on a deeper level than the surface appearance or meaning. Normally, the deeper meaning involves a moral or religious principle. Edmund Spenser's masterpiece *The Faerie Queene*, in which Una represents the British nation and the Recrosse Knight simultaneously symbolizes St. George and Holiness, is the most famous example of an allegory in English literature. Interestingly, there are several other related forms of

allegory, some of which Achebe uses freely, such as the Parable, used primarily to illustrate a religious precept, and the Fable, in which animals are used to demonstrate specific aspects of human nature - there are examples of both these usages in *Things Fall Apart*.

There is a consequent death of the traditional Ibo culture and even the Ibos as a "race" as the tribe members lose their identification with their heritage while becoming absorbed into a world community.

ACHEBE AND EXISTENTIALISM

In *No Longer at Ease* Obi is a prime example of one who no longer belongs. As a result of the events described in *Things Fall Apart*, the alien people have taken over and he is no longer at ease in his culture, his religion, his country - he has been displaced, but nothing concrete has been offered to replace what has been taken from him. This is an especially modern problem, that of those who no longer have any traditional values to fall back upon or to use as guides and who are lost and frustrated in a world that has no meaning to them because they cannot relate to it, just as Obi has a place in neither the disintegrated society of his own people nor the alien British society. The concept of alienation, of man's disharmony with his universe, is the basis of the modern literary movement of existentialism with its major spokesmen Albert Camus (*The Myth of Sisyphus* and *Jean-Paul Sartre* (Existentialism) in France at mid-century. Neither Okonkwo nor Obi finds the existentialist's answer of continually "becoming," however. They cannot "make" themselves, cannot create an "essence" out of their "existence," and as a consequence they are destroyed. Achebe gives no indication that he thinks that the fate of the Ibo people as a whole will be any different, and this may be part of the tragic lesson that he is implying in these two novels.

MASCULINITY/FEMININITY

Directly related to the subject of the breakdown of traditional values and social patterns are Okonkwo's definition of masculinity and Obi's relationship with women. The traditional Ibo society, as exemplified in the figure of Okonkwo in *Things Fall Apart*, is masculine-oriented and controlled. As the prime representative of his people, there is no question that Obi's grandfather was the stern, strong, patriarchal father presiding over a Freudian primal unit. In a society of this sort the woman is an object, something to be treated kindly, but something that is inferior and expected to accede to the desires of the man. (In 1957 the Inter-African Committee report on the role of women documented the subordinate position of African women.) In a sense, the masculine and feminine elements are seen as complementary, two parts of a whole. To be identified with the other gender, however, is demeaning. Obi's peripheral relationships with girls, as illustrated by his concept of love as being a "European invention" prior to his meeting Clara, is pretty much along these lines. He sees the females around him mostly as objects provided to satisfy his needs.

With the breakdown of traditional values and social patterns, however, there is a decided shift from a masculine to a feminine emphasis, perhaps encouraged by the Christian ethic of love, mercy, and tenderness. The traditional, masculine Ibo community has become emasculated and there are no better examples of this than the killing of the sacred python (called "Our Father" by the villagers) in *Things Fall Apart* and a parallel action, the confrontation between Hannah, Obi's mother, and the villagers of Aninta over the beheading of a goat dedicated to the village god Udo in *No Longer at Ease*. In *Things Fall Apart* the action is so unbelievable that the villagers cannot at first comprehend that it was even committed, let alone devise an appropriate punishment for the offender. Obi's mother commits a religious desecration that might have been punished by immediate death at the hands of the villagers in Okonkwo's time. In this case, though, she is punished by nothing more terrifying than threats, because "the emasculation of the clan by the white man's religion and government [had been so successful] that the matter soon died down."

REVERSAL OF ROLES

It is interesting that both Okonkwo's and Obi's fathers are ineffectual. Okonkwo must take over the responsibility of providing for his parents and siblings; it is Obi's mother who determines what will happen in family matters, as in the question of her son's marriage. There has been a reversal, then, of the traditional roles in both novels. Okonkwo overcompensates for his father's failures, shutting out those emotions that might save him, and Obi lacks the masculine strength to stand on his own.

For Achebe, the corruption that characterizes Nigeria in *No Longer at Ease* is a direct result of the loss of identity that comes about with the disintegration of the traditional culture represented in *Things Fall Apart*. As should be evident, then, a careful examination of *No Longer at Ease* is useful for obtaining additional insights into *Things Fall Apart*; although there is no direct organic relationship between the two novels, there are certain facets of the interpretations given above that are enhanced by a knowledge of the later novel that allows for a complete explication and understanding, based on background, and ironic contrasts.

THINGS FALL APART

....

1. Describe Okonkwo's character (i.e., what adjectives would you use?). How does Achebe bring out these qualities in the story? Do you think that Okonkwo's character changes during the course of the novel? Does our perception of him change? Explain.

2. What impact does Okonkwo's childhood have on the rest of his life?

3. What is Okonkwo's fatal flaw? How is this demonstrated?

4. How would you define the concept of family in Okonkwo's culture? What bearing does this concept have on Okonkwo? On other members of his family?

5. Why does Okonkwo commit suicide? Why does Achebe have him commit suicide?

6. Compare and contrast Nwoye and Ikemefuna.

7. Distinguish between Chielo in her role as Priestess of the Oracle of the Hills and Caves and in her everyday village life.

8. Compare and contrast Okonkwo and his grandson (Obi in No Longer at Ease).

9. Many critics contend that Achebe depicts the main conflict in the story as being between the white man and the native African. Do you consider this an accurate analysis? Why or why not? Are the messages contained in *Things Fall Apart* applicable in our society today?

10. How does Okonkwo's life parallel that of his culture?

11. What is the significance of the title of the book being written by the District Commissioner?

12. What is the role of the Oracle of the Hills and Caves in *Things Fall Apart*?

13. Discuss the structure of *Things Fall Apart*. Consider in particular the relationship of the three sections to each other, as well as their comparative lengths.

14. What is the function of the many details of tribal life that Achebe includes in the novel?

15. Comment on Achebe's use of symbolism in *Things Fall Apart*. How, for example, does the incident regarding the holy python reflect the novel's themes?

16. What are the principal turning points in *Things Fall Apart*?

17. Identify the literary **allusions** in *Things Fall Apart* and explain how they function in expressing the **theme** of the novel.

18. Why do you think that *Things Fall Apart* has been so popular throughout the world and over a period of more than thirty years?

19. Discuss the concept of the chi and explain how this affects Okonkwo's life and actions.

20. Okonkwo considers himself a good husband and family man. Do you agree or disagree? Why?

21. Why are ceremonies important in the life of the clan?

22. What is the importance of Nwoye's conversion and change of name?

23. Why is Okonkwo's exile considered such a harsh punishment?

24. Identify the key phrases or lines that you feel sum up the novel and explain your reasoning.

25. Was the District Commissioner justified in using deceit to trap the six leaders from Umuofia? Give examples of African deceit in the novel. What comments about African and European societies might be made in consideration of how deceit is employed in *Things Fall Apart*?

26. Are there any American novels that examine the same **themes** as those in *Things Fall Apart*? Pick one or two and explain how they are alike or dissimilar.

27. What is the role of women in *Things Fall Apart*?

28. Read *Anthills of the Savannahs* and compare and contrast both the **themes** and the style of this latest novel by Achebe with *Things Fall Apart*, his first novel.

29. Examine the film version of *Things Fall Apart*. Is it a true representation of the novel? Explain.

30. What are the major differences between Christianity and Okonkwo's religion? What are the major similarities?

31. What are the differences between how Achebe treats the early twentieth-century villagers' conflict with colonial society in *Arrow of God* and how he treats the similar conflict in *Things Fall Apart*? Do these differences reflect significant thematic differences between the two novels?

32. In what ways is Okonkwo a mythic hero? In what ways is he an Aristotelian hero?

33. Corruption is a major force in contemporary Nigerian life. Are there any clues in *Things Fall Apart* that would indicate why this is so?

34. Do you think that it is appropriate and valid to consider *Things Fall Apart* in terms of Aristotelian tragedy? Explain your reasoning.

35. Examine the reaction to critics to *Things Fall Apart*. What conclusions can you draw about the novel, Achebe, the critics, and/or the reading public based upon your study?

36. How does Achebe utilize **foreshadowing**, **irony**, symbolism, and other literary devices in *Things Fall Apart*?

37. Are there any parallels between the use of wrestling in Okonkwo's society and in contemporary America? What significance do you attach to this fact?

38. What function do proverbs and folktales serve in *Things Fall Apart*?

39. Why did Achebe include two white missionaries in his tale instead of just one?

40. How does the final paragraph in the novel sum up the book?

41. Can the four levels of interpretations of *Things Fall Apart* be reconciled?

42. Why aren't the secondary characters fully developed?

43. Discuss Achebe's use of language as a political statement and/or a stylistic device.

44. Would *Things Fall Apart* have been more effective if related by a first-person narrator? Explain.

45. What sorts of evidence can you find in the novel that demonstrate Achebe's non-African experiences, including his educational background?

46. Explore the subject of slavery in Africa before the arrival of the white man.

47. Read and analyze some of Achebe's writings for children. How do these compare with his adult novels?

48. Examine Achebe's political and artistic articles (and interviews). How well do his novels represent the theories that he states in his essays? Is the writer more effective as a novelist or as an essayist? Explain your conclusion.

49. How does the Ibo attitude toward death, murder, and related concepts compare with that of your society?

50. How is the breakdown of traditional values and social patterns related to gender identification in *Things Fall Apart*?

51. Read novels by John Pepper Clark, Amos Tutuola, James Ngugi, Mongo Beti, Ousame Soce Diop, Cameron Duodu, T. M. Aluka, and Cyprian Ekwensi, among others. What, if any, common elements do you find in their works? How do they compare and relate to Achebe and vice versa?

BIBLIOGRAPHY

· ·

PRIMARY SOURCES: WRITINGS BY CHINUA ACHEBE

Novels

Things Fall Apart. London: Heinemann, 1958; rpt. African Writers Series, No. 1, 1962; rpt. New York: Fawcett, 1959; rpt. New York: McDonald, Obolensky, 1959; rpt. New York: Fawcett, 1977.

No Longer at Ease, London: Heinemann, 1960; rpt. New York: Obolensky 1960; rpt. New York: Fawcett, 1961; rpt. African Writers Series, No. 3, 1963.

Arrow of God. London: Heinemann, 1964; rpt. African Writers Series, No. 16, 1965; rpt. New York: John Day, 1967.

A Man of the People. London: Heinemann, 1966. African Writers Series, No. 31. rpt. New York: John Day, 1966.

Anthills of the Savannah. London: Heinemann, 1987; rpt. New York: Anchor/ Doubleday, 1988.

Short Stories

Girls at War. London: Heinemann, 1972. African Writers Series, No. 100. rpt. New York: Doubleday, 1973.

The Sacrificial Egg and Other Stories. Onitsha, Nigeria: Etudo, 1962. Five short stories written between 1952 and 1960.

Editor. *The Insider: Stories of War and Peace from Nigeria*. Enugu, Nigeria: Nwankwo-Ifejika, Chatham Bookseller, 1971.

With C. L. Innes. *African Short Stories*. London: Heinemann, 1985.

Poetry

Beware Soul-Brother: Poems. Nigeria: Nwanko-Ifejika, 1971; rpt. London: Heinemann, 1972 (rev.).

Christmas in Biafra and Other Poems. New York: Doubleday, 1973.

Children's Stories

Chike and the River. Cambridge, England: Cambridge University Press, 1966. Children's novel.

The Drum. Nigeria: Fourth Dimension, 1977; rpt. in Wonders, ed. Jonathan Cott and Mary Gimbel, Summit Books, 1980.

"The Flute." In *Sharing Literature with Children*, ed. Francelia Butler. New York: David McKay, 1977.

With John Iroaganachi. *How the Leopard Got His Claws*. Enugu, Nigeria: Nwanko-Ifejika, 1972. Bound with *Lament of the Deer*, by Christopher Okigbo, Third Press, 1973.

Essays

"English and the African Writer." *Transition*, No. 18, 1965; rpt. Insight, October/December 1966, pp. 19–21.

"Foreword." In *Selection of African Prose*, ed. W. H. Whiteley, Vol. I: Traditional Oral Texts. Oxford: Oxford University Press, 1964.

Hopes and Impediments: *Selected Essays, 1956–1987*. London: Heinemann, 1987; rpt. New York: Doubleday, 1989.

Esther Terry, Michael Thelwell, and John Wideman. "James Baldwin, 1924–1987." *The Massachusetts Review*, Vol. 28 (Winter, 1987): 551.

Morning Yet on Creation Day. New York: Doubleday, 1975.

"On Janheinz Hahn and Exekiel Mphahlele." *Transition*, 8, 1963. Literary theory.

"The Black Writer's Burden." *Presence Africaine*, 1962.

"The Novelist as Teacher." *New Statesman*, 29, January 1965, p. 162.

"The Role of the Writer in a New Nation." *Nigeria Magazine*, No. 81, June 1964, pp. 158–160. "The Trouble with Nigeria." 1984.

"Where Angels Fear to Tread." *Nigeria Magazine*, No. 75, 1962.

Primary Sources: Interviews With Chinua Achebe

"English and the African Writer." *Transition*, IV, 18 (1965): 27–30

"The Novelist as Teacher." *Commonwealth Literature*, ed. John Press. London: Heinmann, 1965.

"The Black Writer's Burden." *Presence Africaine*, (English Edition), 31 (1966): 135–40.

'The African Writer and the Biafran Cause." *Conch*, Vol. I, no. 1 (March 1969): 8–14.

"Chinua Achebe on Biafra." *Transition*, 36, 1968. Emenyonu, Ernest and Pat Emenyonu. "Interview with Chinua Achebe." *Africa Report*, May 1972, pp. 21, 23, 25–27.

Jeyifo, Biodun. "The Author's Art." *World Press Review*, Vol. 32 (January, 1985): 58, ff. rpt.

Nwachukwu-Agbada, J. O. J. "An Interview with Chinua Achebe." *The Massachusetts Review*, Vol. 28 (Summer, 1987): 273, ff.

Serumaga, Robert. "Interview with Achebe." *Cultural Events in Africa*, No. 28. London, Transcription Centre, 1967.

Secondary Sources

Abrahams, Cecil. "Margaret Laurence and Chinua Achebe: Commonwealth Storytellers." *ACLALS Bulletin*, Vol. 5, no. 3 (1980): 74–85. A comparison of the two novelists.

Adejumo, M. S. and Oladapo Adelusi. *Notes and Essays on Chinua Achebe's Things Fall Apart*. Adejumo, M.S.; Ibadan: Onibonoje, 1966.

Aragbabalu, Omidiji (pseudonym for Ulli Beier). "Review of No Longer at Ease." *Black Orpheus*, 8, p. 51.

Breskina, F. "Traditionalisme et modernisme, Metamophose d'une Theorie." In *Essays on African Culture*. Ed. M. A. Korostovstsev, trans. Vitaman, Lmovervozu, and Biryukov. Moscow: Central Department of Oriental Studies; Nakua, 1966. Pp. 120–137. In French.

Carrol, David. *Chinua Achebe*. New York: Twayne, 1970. A good introductory overview.

Cartey, Wilfred. *Whispers from a Continent*. New York: Random House, 1969.

Clark, John Pepper. "The Legacy of Caliban." *Black Orpheus*, Vol. II, no. i, 1968. Includes discussion of Achebe's use of language.

Cook, David. *African Literature: A Critical View*. London: Longman, 1977. Includes "The Centre Holds" (pp. 65–81), a short, useful chapter that attempts to create an analytical synthesis to show how in *Things Fall Apart* the whole is greater than the sum of its parts.

Cott, Jonathan. *Pipers at the Gates of Dawn: The Wisdom of Children's Literature*. New York: Random House, 1981. Includes a discussion of Achebe's writings for juveniles.

Daily, Christophe. "The Novelist as a Cultural Policy Maker." *Presence Africaine: Cultural Review of the Negro World*, 125 (1983), pp. 202–213.

Duerden, Dennis and Cosmo Pieterse, eds. *African Writers Talking*. London: Heinemann, 1972.

Ezuma, Ben. *Questions and Answers on Things Fall Apart with List of Suggested Questions, Phrases and Difficult Words Fully Explained*. Onitsha, Nigeria: Tabansi Bookshop, n.d.

Gleason, Judith, I. "Out of the **Irony** of Words. " *Transition*, No. 18, 1965.

- This Africa: Northwestern University Press, Evanston, 1965. Gowda, H. H. Annian. "Ahmed Ali's Twilight in Delhi and Chinua Achebe's *Things Fall Apart.*" In *Alien Voice: Perspectives on Commonwealth Literature.* Lucknow: Print House, 1981; rpt. Atlantic Highlands, N. J.: Humanities, 1982. A comparison of the two novels.

Granquvist, Raoul. "The Early Swedish Reviews of Chinua Achebe's *Things Fall Apart* and *A Man of the People.*" *Research in African Literatures*, Vol. 15, no. 3 (Fall, 1984): 394–404. Swedish reactions to the novel.

Green, R. "The Clashing of Old and New." *The Nation*, Vol. CCL, no. II, 1965.

Heywood, Christopher, ed. *Perspectives on African Literature.* London: Heinemann; rpt. New York: Africana, 1972.

Irele, Abiola. "The Tragic Conflict in Achebe's Novels." *Black Orpheus*, No. 17 (1965): 27–32; rpt. in *Introduction to African Literature*, ed. Ulli Beier, London: Longmans, 1967.

Ivasheva, V. V. "Roman sovremennoj Nigerii." In *Literatura stran Afriki.* Moscow: Nauka, 1964. Pp. 39–74. Soviet/Marxist criticism.

JanMohamed, Abdul. "Sophisticated Primitivism: The Syncretism of Oral and Literate Modes in Achebe's *Things Fall Apart. Ariel*, Vol. 15, no. 4 (October, 1984): 19–39.

Jones, Eldred. "Jungle Drums and Wailing Pianos: West African Fiction and Poetry in English." *African Forum*, Vol. 1, no. 4, 1966, pp. 93–106.

"Language and **Theme** in *Things Fall Apart.*" *Review of English Literature*, Vol. 5, no, 4 (1964): 39–43.

Kar, Prafulla O. "The Image of the Vanishing African in Chinua Achebes Novels." In *The Colonial and Neo-Colonial Encounters in Commonwealth Literature*, ed. H. H. Annian Gowda. Mysore: Prasarasana University Press, 1983.

Kayondo, Frances Sales. "Chinua Achebe, *Things Fall Apart* as a Source for Education in Human Values in Africa." *Dissertation Abstracts International*, Vol. 48, no. 1 (July, 1987): 37A.

Killam, G. D[ouglas]. *Africa in English Fiction*, 1874–1939. Ibadan: Ibadan University Press, 1968.

-Ed. *African Writers on African Writing*. London: Heinmann, 1973. An excellent reference source.

-*The Novels of Chinua Achebe*. London: Heinemann, 1969; New York: Africana, 1969. A good, traditional examination of Achebe's writing.

Kirpal, Viney. "*Things Fall Apart*: A Colonial Novel." *The Literary Endeavor*, Vol. 4, nos. 1–2 (July-December, 1982): 33–38.

Klima, Vladimir. *Modern Nigerian Novels*. Prague: Academia 1969. An excellent overall introduction.

Larson, Charles R. *The Emergence of African Fictions*. Rev. ed. Bloomington: Indiana University Press, 1972. One drawback to this study is that in his interpretation of *Things Fall Apart* Larson fails to take into account Achebe's knowledge of Western civilization and his exposure to the concept of Aristotelian tragedy.

-"The Film Version of Achebe's *Things Fall Apart*." *Africana Journal*, Vol. 13, nos. 1–4 (1982): 104–110.

Laurence, Margaret. *Long Drums and Cannons: Nigerian Dramatists and Novelists*. London: Macmillan, 1968; rpt. New York: Praeger, 1968. One of the standard studies of the subject. Of Achebe she says, whether a "portrayal of the Old society ... [or] of a contemporary society in the throes of transition" there is "one **theme** which runs through everything [that Achebe] has written - human communication and the lack of it."

Lindfors, Bernth. "The Palm Oil with which Achebe's Words Are Eaten." *African Literature Today*, I, 1968. Discusses Achebe's use of language, focusing on **imagery** in the novels. Includes a good discussion of the novelist's use of proverbial materials.

McCarthy, B. Eugene. "Rhythm and Narrative Method in Achebe's *Things Fall Apart*." *Novel*, Vol. 18, no. 3 (Spring, 1985): 243–256.

McDougall, Russell. "Okonkwo's Walk: The Choreography of *Things Fall Apart*." *World Literature Written in English*, Vol. 26, no. 1 (Spring, 1986): 24–33.

MacLeod, A. L. *The Commonwealth Pen: An Introduction to The Literature of the British Commonwealth*. Ithaca: Cornell University Press, 1961.

Madubuike, Ihechukwu. "Achebe's Ideas on Literature." *Black World*, December, 1974, pp. 60–69. An overview of the writer's work, with attention to his relationship to the Onitsha Market Literature and including interview materials.

Maduka, Chidi T. "African Religious Beliefs in Literary Imagination: Agbanje and Abiku in Chinua Achebe, J.P. Clark and Wole Soyinka." *The Journal of Commonwealth Literature*, Vol. 22, no. 1 (1987): 17–30.

Meyers, Jeffrey. "Culture and History in *Things Fall Apart*." *Critique: Studies in Modern Fiction*, 11, (1969): 33–41.

Moore, Gerald. "English Words. African Lives." *Presence Africaine*, No. 54, 1965.

Moore, Gerald. *Seven African Writers*. Oxford: Oxford University Press, Three Crowns Series, 1962.. Shows good insights.

-The Chosen Tongue. London: Longmans, 1969. Nandakumar, P. The Glory and the Good:" *Essays in Literature*. New Delhi, 1965. Contains a chapter on Achebe.

Ngugi, James. "**Satire** in Nigeria." *In Protest and Conflict in African Literature*, ed. Cosmo Pieterse and Donal Munro. London: Heinemann, 1969. Pp. 56–69. Of very limited value.

Nkosi, Lewis. "Interview with Lewis Nkosi." *African Report*, Vol. IX, no. vii. Washington, D.C.: African American Institute, July 1964. p. 20; rpt. in *Commonwealth Literature*, ed. John Press. London: Heinemann, 1965. Interview with Achebe.

Nnolim, Charles E. "The Form and Function of Tradition in Achebe's Novels." *Ariel*, Vol. 14, no. 1 (1983): 35–47.

Olorounto, Samuel Boladji. "The Notion of Conflict in Chinua Achebe's Novels." *Obsidian II*, Vol. 1, no. 3 (Winter, 1968): 17–36.

"The Significance of Growing Up in Selected Novels of Chinua Achebe, Camara Laye, Cheikh Hamidou Kane and Ngugi wa Thiong'o." *Dissertation Abstracts International*, Vol. 41, no. 11 (May, 1981): 4711A.

Opata, Damian U. "Eternal Sacred Order versus Conventional Wisdom: A Consideration of Moral Culpability in the Killing of Ikemefuna in *Things Fall Apart*." *Research in African Literatures*, Vol. 10, no. 1 (Spring, 1987): 71–79.

Osbaa, Kalu. "A Cultural Note on Okonkwo's Suicide." *Kunapipi*, Vol. 3, no. 2 (1981): 126–134.

Palmer, Eustace. *An Introduction to the African Novel*. London: Heinemann; rpt. New York: Africana, 1972. A well-balanced interpretation, with good insights into Achebe's obvious strengths as a writer, but with attention to his novelistic weaknesses as well. Does not romanticize African tribal life, seeing in it many of the same failures as appear in Western societies.

Peters, Jonathan A. *A Dance of Masks: Senghor, Achebe, Soyinka*. Washington, D. C.: Three Continents, 1978. Includes a chapter on *Things Fall Apart*, "From Culture to Anarchy" (pp. 93–114), which, while a little short, is insightful.

Press, John, ed. *Commonwealth Literature*. London: Heinemann, 1965.

Puhr, Kathleen M. "Things Come Together with *Things Fall Apart*." *English Journal*, Vol. 76 (November, 1987): 43–44. A brief description of a high school teaching unit that includes *Things Fall Apart*, which is seen as a legitimate and straightforward way to introduce students to elements of a "foreign" culture that parallel the "legacy of tragedy to such familiar writers as Euripides and Shakespeare."

Ramsaran, John A. "English Writing in West Africa." In *Approaches to African Literature*. Ibadan, 1959.

Ravenscroft, Arthur. "African Literature V: Novels of Disillusion." The *Journal of Commonwealth Literature*, No. 5, 1968.

Chinua Achebe. London: Longmans, 1969. *Writers and Their Work Series*, No. 209. Oversimplified introduction composed mainly of plot summaries.

Serumaga, Robert. " A Mirror for Integration." In *Protest and Conflict in African Literature*. Cosmo Pieterse and Donald Munro, eds. London: Heinemann, 1969. Pp. 70–80. Of very limited value.

Shelton, Austin J. "The Offended Chi in Achebe's Novels." *Transition*, No. 13, 1964.

Simms, Norman. "Noetics and Poetics: Studying and Appreciating Chinua Achebe's *Things Fall Apart.*" *Chandrabhasa*, 5 (Summer, 1981): 57–66.

Soyinka, Wole. "And After the Narcissist?" *African Forum*, Vol. 1, no. 4 (1966): 53–64.

Stock, A. G. "Yeats and Achebe." *The Journal of Commonwealth Literature*, No. 5, 1968.

Taiwo, Oladele. *An Introduction to West African Literature*. London: Nelson, 1967.

Taylor, Willene P. "The Search for Values **Theme** in Chinua Achebe's Novel *Things Fall Apart*: A Crisis of the Soul." *Griot*, Vol. 2, no. 2 (Summer, 1983): 17–26.

Tibble, Anne. *African/English Literature*. Austin: October Press, 1965.

Traore, Ousseynou. "Aesthetic Ideology and Oral Narrative Paradigms in *Things Fall Apart* and *Arrow of God.*" *Dissertation Abstracts International*, Vol. 42, no. 10 (April, 1982): 4448A.

Veselkin, E. A. "The African Personality." In *Essays on African Culture*, ed. M. A. Korostovstsev, translated by Vitaman, Lmovervozu, and Biryukov. Moscow: Central Department of Oriental Studies; Nakua, 1966: 72–93.

Washmare, J. M. "Chinua Achebe's Vision of the Crumbling Past." In *Indian Readings in Commonwealth Literature*, ed. G. S. Amur, V. R. N. Prasad, B. V. Nemade, and N. H. Nihalani. New York: Sterling, 1985.

Wasserman, Julian N. "The Sphinx and the Rough Beast: Linguistic Struggle in Chinua Achebe's *Things Fall Apart*." *Mississippi Folklore Register*, Vol. 16, no. 2 (Fall, 1982): 61–70.

Wauthier, Claude. *The Literature and Thought of Modern Africa*. London: Pall Mall Press, 1966.

Weinstock, Donald J. and Cathy Ramadan. "Symbolic Structure in *Things Fall Apart*." *Critique*, 11 (1969): 33–41. Includes commentary on Achebe's use of Ibo proverbs and stories, which the authors see as an important and effective device for **foreshadowing** important plot events and in emphasizing the novel's central themes.

Wren, Robert A. Achebe's *World: The Historical and Cultural Context of Chinua Achebe's Novels*. Washington, D. C.: Three Continents, 1980.

Winters, Marjorie. "An Objective Approach Achebe's Style." *Research in African Literatures*, Vol. 12, no. 1 (Spring, 1981): 55–68. See also "An Objective Approach to the Style of Chinua Achebe" in *Winters' Toward Defining the African Aesthetic*, Washington, D. C.: Three Continents, 1982.

Zell, Hans M. and Helena Silver. *A Reader's Guide to African Literature*. London: Heinemann, 1972. An extremely useful reference book filled with biographies of the most important African authors, critiques of their works, and pertinent book publishers and journals' addresses.

USEFUL BACKGROUND MATERIAL

Adedeji, J. A. "The Origin of the Yoruba Masque Theatre: The Use of Ifa Divination Corpus as Historical Evidence." *African Notes*, VI, 1, (1970), 70–86.

Afigbo, A. E. *The Warrant Chiefs: Indirect Rule in Southeastern Nigeria*, 1891–1929. London: Longman, 1972.

Aje, S. O. "Metamorphosis and Artistic Function of Objects in African Literature." *Neochelicon*, Vol. 10, no. 1 (1983): 239–249.

Anozie, Lynda. "Semantic-Pragmatic Analysis of an Igbo Metaphorical Proverb." In *Phenomenology in Modern African Studies*. Owerri: Conch Magazine, 1982.

Bascom, William R. and Melville J. Herskovits. *Continuity and Change in African Cultures*. Chicago: University of Chicago Press, 1959.

Beier, Ulli, ed. *Introduction to African Literature: An Anthology of Critical Writing from Black Orpheus*. London: Longman's, 1967.

Bolaji, Labanji. *Anatomy of Corruption in Nigeria*. Ibadan: Daystar Press, 1970.

Crowder, Michael. *West African Resistance: The Military Response to Colonial Occupation*. London: Hutchinson, 1971.

Dailly, Christophe. "The Novelist as a Cultural Policy-Maker." *Presence Africaine*, 125 (1983): 202–213.

Fage, J. D. *An Atlas of African History*. London: Arnold Press, 1970.

Glifford, Prosser and William Roger Louis, eds. *France and Britain in Africa: Imperial Rivalry and Colonial Rule*. New Haven: Yale University Press, 1971.

Green, M. M. *Ibo Village Affairs*. New York: Praeger, 1964.

Idowu, B. E. *Olodumare: God in Yoruba Belief*. New York: Praeger, 1963.

Iloegbunam, Chuks. "Nigeria's Faulkner." Newswatch, March 24, 1986; rpt. *World Press Review*, Vol. 33 (June, 1986): 56–57. Very brief overview of Achebe's novelistic career.

Kimble, George H. T. *Tropical Africa*. New York: Twentieth Century Fund, 1960.

Labouret, Henri. *Africa Before the White Man*. New York: Walker, 1962.

Lewis, Maureen Warner. "Ezeulu and His God." *Black World*, December, 1974: 71–87. Although an analysis of Achebe's *Arrow of God*, this article includes passing commentary on *Things Fall Apart*.

Lugard, Lord. *The Dual Mandate in British Tropical Africa*. Fifth Edition. London: Frank Cass, 1965.

Mannoni, Dominique. *O Prospero and Caliban: The Psychology of Colonization*. New York: Praeger, 1964.

Mbiti, John S. *African Religions and Philosophy*. New York: Doubleday, 1970.

Memmi, Albert. *The Colonizer and the Colonized*. Translated from the French. Boston: Orion, 1965.

Moore, Clark D. and Ann Dunbar, eds. *Africa Yesterday and Today*. New York: Bantam, 1968. A quick-reference book on all aspects of Africa; composed mainly of extracts from histories, scientific studies, and political writings.

Morris, Peter. *African City Life*. [Kampala]: Transition Press, [1968].

Nwoga, Donatus. "The Chi Offended." *Transition*, Vol. IV, no. 15 (1964): 5.

Obumselu, Ben. "The Background of Modern African Literature." *Ibadan*, 22, (June, 1966): 46–59.

Ojelabi, Adekunle. *A Textbook of West African History: 1000 A.D. to the Present Day*. Ibadan: Education Research Institute, 1970 (c. 1971).

Robinson, Ronald, and others. *Africa and the Victorians: The Official Mind of Imperialism*. London: MacMillan, 1961.

Smith, Edwin. *The Golden Stool: Some Aspects of the Conflict of Cultures in Africa*. London: Holborn, 1927.

Wallerstein, Immanuel. *Africa: The Politics of Independence*. New York: Random House, 1961.

Note

Biographical information and representative critical responses to Achebe's writing are available in a wide variety of reference sources such as *Contemporary Literary Criticism* (Volumes 1,3,5,7,11,26), *Current Biography*, *Contemporary Authors New Revision* Series (vol. 6), *Contemporary Authors* (vol. 1–4R), *Contemporary Poets* (1980), *Contemporary Novelists* (1982), *Something About the Author* (vols. 38, 40), and *Twentieth-Century Children's Writers* (2nd ed., 1983). Reference works that focus on African writers include *African Writers, Penguin Companion to Classical, Oriental* and *African Literature, Who's Who in African Literature*, and *World Bibliography of African Bibliographies*. Although somewhat dated, *Black African Literature in English: A Guide to Information Sources*, Bernth Linfors (Ed.; Detroit: Gale, 1979, Vol. 23 of the Gale Information Guide Library), *African Authors* (Black Orpheus Press, 1973), *Africa South of the Sahara* (Europa Publications, 1978), *A Reader's Guide to African Literature* (Hans M. Zell and Helene Silver; New York: Africana, 1971), *Black African Literature in English since 1952, Works and Criticism* (Barbara Abrash; New York: Johnson, 1967), and *African Literature: A Student's Guide to Reference Resources* (Montreal: McLennan Library, McGill University Press, 1977; ERIC no.: ED 096 942) provide an interesting background and historical perspective and are worth consulting. Among the scholarly journals that specialize in African topics are *African Literature Today* (annual; includes an international bibliography of African writing in books and periodicals) and *Research in African Literatures* (quarterly). Students should also examine the *Journal of Commonwealth Literature, World Literature Today*, and *World Literature Written in English*. Additional general sources of information include the *Reader's Guide to Periodical Literature* (monthly), the *Modern Language Association's MLA International Bibliography* (annual), *Abstracts of English Studies* (monthly, September through July), *Annual Bibliography of English Language and Literature, Arts and Humanities Citation Index* (three times a year), *Book Review Digest* (monthly), *Book Review Index* (bimonthly), *British Humanities Index* (annual), *Cumulative Book Index* (annual), *Dissertations Abstracts International* (monthly), *English Studies* ("Current Literature" section), *Humanities Index* (quarterly), *Index to Theses* (London: Aslib; annual), *Journal of Modern Literature* ("Annual Bibliography - February issue), *The New York Times Index* (biweekly), *The Times Index* (London; annual), *Twentieth Century Literature* ("Current Bibliography" - October issue), and *The Year's Work in English Studies* (annual).